Mission:

motherhood

by **Mrs. Cathy Corle**

Revival Fires! Publishing
P.O. Box 245
Claysburg, PA 16625
(814) 239-2813

printed in the United States of America

Mission: motherhood

Introduction

Dear Friends and Fellow-Moms!

It's been tempting to say I want to stick with more 'spiritual' topics, and shy away from one as down-to-earth and day-to-day as motherhood until after my children are grown. If I did that, I would plan to let out my big sigh of relief once I've seen that my on-going 'projects' have become completed masterpieces, and not be so reticent about lending any advice or encouragement to others who wear the title of 'MOM' before I know the final outcome of my own life's work.

But I see so many moms needing an encouraging word, or even just the reassurance that other mothers are fighting the same battles that they are facing. We're all in this together, and we need to 'exhort one another, and so much more as we see the day approaching.' The closer we come to the return of Christ, the harder the devil fights against us in all of our endeavors to serve and please the Lord, especially those areas that involve building a godly home and raising children in the nurture and admonition of the Lord, with the prayer that they will grow to be adults who will live for the glory and service of the King of kings.

So I've rounded up several of the articles that I've written specifically for moms over the years and kind of watched myself grow up as a mother by rereading these messages from the past. The very first one appeared in the small newsletter called "Revival Fires" that later grew into a nation-wide publication. The Ministry of Mothering was the very first Helps for the Helpmeet article in the very first issue of the very first form of Revival Fires, that I worked so hard to put together on an ancient typewriter when I was a very young preacher's wife with two children aged three years and three months. My, that was a long time ago!

The Ark that Jochebed Built is another one from those early motherhood years. While I still had so much to learn in terms of real life, I'm thankful when I look back on those thoughts that my ideals and goals were high ones, that my desire and aim as a new mom was to raise my children for the glory of God, and to challenge others to do the same.

In some of the more recent messages like Another Look at the Ministry of Mom and Success in Motherhood, I find myself sounding more down to earth, and I'm seeing and feeling more of the need for encouragement and assurance for moms. I've learned that both ends of the spectrum are important, so here it all is.

Please have mercy on the far-from-perfect mom who wrote and compiled these thoughts. This is far from a how-to-do-it manual. I only want to be a blessing and encouragement. I trust that something in these pages will help you to laugh a little, and know that there is Someone standing by to hear and to care when you just have to cry. Whatever need we have, whatever problem we face, whatever wisdom is necessary in fulfilling the role of mother in the family where we serve, we can trust that it's available to us in the Word of God and in prayer.

We're so blessed to have the calling of God upon our lives to help point young lives in the right direction of bringing glory to God, and to have His promises of guidance and strength and wisdom to meet every need and every test.

Thank you for sharing the thoughts in this book with me. I trust that something in these pages will be a blessing.

Because of Jesus,

Cathy Corle

Chapter One

The Ministry of Mothering

"...Take heed to the ministry which thou hast received of the Lord, that thou fulfill it." (Colossians 4:17)

During the month of May we mothers have allowed our families to lavish praise on us for our labor and enjoyed gifts and cards in honor of being mothers. Being a mother is certainly a 24-hour-a-day job for which the rewards cannot be measured in a weekly paycheck. Now that we have been so honored, I would like to challenge you to join me in examining our ministry as mothers.

Just what is the motivation you have in child-rearing? For some it is the desire to enjoy their children. Others desire someone to love and to love them in return. Some rear children so that they will have someone for companionship and security in their old age. These are natural results of proper mothering, but not acceptable to God as a motivating ideal.

The best reason for child-rearing, and the reason God gave children to us to raise, is so that we can bring glory to God through their lives. When examined in this light,

1

perhaps there are some things we need to change. Our schedule? Our priorities? What about the dreams and aspirations that we have for their future? These are all very important if God is to receive glory through their lives.

Hannah had this proper motivation when she bore a son named Samuel. ***"...If thou...wilt give unto thine handmaid a manchild, then I will give him unto the Lord all the days of his life..."*** *(1 Samuel 1:11)*

Jochebed shared this purpose when the Lord gave her a son named Moses. Both of these ladies only had their sons during infancy and early childhood, yet the training they had already received in that short time-span produced in them the character and convictions that resulted in their faithful service to God; each of these men was the primary spokesman for God in his lifetime! We have 18 years in which to mold character and instill principle. Are we being as faithful to our responsibility to give godly training to our precious children?

I believe very strongly in the vital role of fathers in training and teaching children, yet the Bible shares with us encouraging examples of ladies who were successful in rearing godly children without the support of a spiritual father. Such is the case of Eunice, the mother of Timothy, who faithfully taught the Scriptures to her son when he was a small child. (2 Timothy 1:5; 3:15)

In 2 Kings chapter 18, we find that Hezekiah was more obedient to God than any of the kings before him despite the fact that his father Ahaz was one of the most wicked kings in Judah's history. Probably, his mother Abi was faithful in her task as a ministering mother, and God honored it in the life of her son.

How many of our best ladies regularly go door-to-door with the Gospel and then we fail to share it with our own little ones? How many diligently teach the Bible to the children at Sunday School and never teach the Bible to the children at home? Are we consistently begging God to save their souls and keep their hearts and minds pure? Rest assured, no one is going to care enough to pray for them any more than mother does. Let's not neglect to plead with God in their behalf.

Children have so many physical needs to make demands on our time that their spiritual needs can easily slip by us unnoticed. Our greatest privilege as mothers is to lead our little ones to Jesus Christ. This is the primary way in which we may fulfill our ministry as mothers, to be as much a part of their second birth as we were in their first! Our children need to be discipled and encouraged to grow in Christ as much as any other baby Christian, and we have a wonderful opportunity for this in the home. How sad for the Christian mother to leave this responsibility to the folks at church and miss one of the greatest blessings that God has in store for her.

A second way for us to minister is to teach them that every part of their lives are important to God. How precious for our children to come to us with their hurts and worries to ask us to pray. If we want them to do so when they are older, we must teach them that they can while they are small. It is up to us to make Christianity livable and practicable to our children. The principles and convictions they will have as adults depend on the teaching and example they receive from us while they are children.

It has been said many times: "The hand that rocks the cradle rules the world." Most certainly then, the mother that ministers can have immeasurable influence on things to come. As we serve God in the various ministries for which He gives us opportunity, let's be sure to fulfill our ministry at home as well.

Every bruised knee, every shared blessing, and every

disobedience corrected is a big opportunity for the ministering mother. Let us "take heed" to our ministry as mothers so that we can fulfill it.

Chapter Two

The Ark That Jochebed Built

"And when she could not longer hide him, she took for him an ark of bulrushes, and daubed it with slime and with pitch, and put the child therein; and she laid it in the flags by the river's brink." (Exodus 2:3)

Years ago when my children were very small I wrote this message for Mother's Day. Not long ago I had it on my mind, and knew that I need to be reminded of the decisions that I made and the beliefs that I held high, and check myself once again to see where I have allowed things to slip. Since I needed it, I'm sure that someone else does, too. Maybe it will be the reminder that we need to get back on track if we've gotten away from protecting our children's hearts and lives and futures in the midst of a wicked world.

5

Mission: Motherhood

There are three arks recorded in Scripture. The ark that Noah built was an ark of deliverance and salvation. (Genesis 6) The ark that Bezaleel built was an ark of covenant and promise that carried proof of God's provision for His beloved people. (Exodus 37:1) The ark that Jochebed built was the evidence of a mother's undying love and watchcare for her treasured child.

In the opening chapters of Exodus we find a heart-touching story of mother and child. She was born under oppression of godless powers, and brought children into the world under that same bondage. She and her husband had lost all of their freedoms and the fruits of their labor as the rule of the wicked Pharaoh continually became more oppressive. Now he would presume to take even their precious children and cast them helplessly into the savage waters of the Nile.

But there was one thing that even Pharaoh failed to take account of, and that was the faith, endurance, strength, ingenuity and undying love found in a mother's heart.

I would like to make an analogy between the situation of this mother, and the predicament that mothers face in today's world. Egypt is always symbolic of the world's system, and the ruler of this world is the devil himself. The Nile was the life-line and the central point of activity in wicked Egypt. Like Jochebed, mothers today face a threat just as menacing, the very real possibility of losing their children to the world and the devil. We need to pause and consider the seriousness of its nature.

First, She Hid Him.

We cannot afford to underestimate the constant invitation and indoctrination with which Satan daily confronts our little ones. The occult training on the Saturday morning cartoons, the rock music culture, the rebellion and violence of television, drugs, the humanistic philosophies in our schools and colleges all have our children pre-programmed for the devil's purposes before they ever get to church for a few hours during the week. Unless some godly mothers intervene, our children will be lost just as literally as those who were cast into the Nile long ago.

Consider the fact that soon Jochebed would have to carefully place her child in the same place where Pharaoh had desired to toss him. The Nile was the livelihood in Egypt. The devil desires to throw our children helpless into the midst of the world's life-line and watch with glee as they flounder desperately and are lost.

I am so weary of hearing people say, "You can't shelter your children forever... They have to live in the world and face it someday." How foolish! Do you allow your baby to crawl into a rattlesnake pit, because he is going to have to learn to watch out for them anyway? Do you let your two-year-old play on the interstate so he will learn to watch for cars? If your only approach to teaching them about danger is pushing them into the midst of it, they won't survive long enough to have learned the lesson.

The people who would instantly accuse us of criminal neglect if we were to make such a serious error with physical dangers are the same ones who discourage us from properly protecting our children from spiritual dangers. Our children do have to live in the world, just like they have to learn to watch for cars. But before they should be abandoned on their own, they need the protection and training of parents who love them, and the chance to mature and formulate ideals and principles that will guide them through the perils of the world.

Mission: Motherhood

A wise mother who truly loves the children God has loaned to her will not allow her little ones to be prematurely cast into the world before they know right from wrong, and before they have developed spiritual strength. First Jochebed hid her little son from the threat of the Nile, and there is a time in the life of every child when we should do the same.

Then, She Prepared The Ark

Realizing the danger her child was in, Jochebed set out to change the outcome of the story. In secret she began to prepare the vessel that would save her child's life. Though she would still have to let him go into the same perilous waters, she vowed to make a way that her child could be in the midst of the river, and yet remain untouched by it. By God's grace, we must see that our children's lives are prepared to go into the world without being destroyed by the world.

The Scripture says that she 'took for him an ark'. She took for her purpose something that was already at her disposal which was made of something readily available. Not every mother has a great store of money, talent, or education to aid her in rescuing her child from the devil, but there is something that every mother does have in plentiful supply, and that is a mother's love.

No gift of giving self, without one doubt,
Can better illustrate the gift of Christ,
Than mother, who in silence does without
For her child's good --
A Mother's Sacrifice.

8

The Ark That Jochebed Built

No one except the Lord who intercedes
More diligently solicits God's great care,
Than that sweet, sainted soul
On bended knee
Who begs in their behalf --
A Mother's Prayer.

No truer picture men will ever see
Of what's within the heart of God above,
Than the one whose love will
Reach out endlessly -
Her child cannot outlive --
A MOTHER'S LOVE.

Such love, in some measure, is potentially hidden away in the heart of every woman who is called 'Mother'. No matter how hurt or disappointed, no matter how deeply buried beneath other cares and concerns, a mother's love is always available, ever accessible.

Though only God knows the exact formulation, mother-love is made up of alot of little things we know something about. A list of ingredients might include some things like:... that seizing panic that grips her heart when her child faces danger... the certainty that her child is the brightest, handsomest, most talented in the lot... those worrisome tears that often slide silently down her cheeks and into the dishpan...

The frequent inability to sleep at night due to a small child's fever... 16,000 home-cooked meals... 8,400 loads of laundry... 999 trips to the doctor, dentist, orthodontist, optometrist, and hospital... countless school plays, ball games, piano lessons, choir practices, and church activities for which the chauffeur is always (of course) Mom... the consuming desire for them to have every opportunity that she missed... the silent hope that no matter how far into sin they go or how much wrong they do, there is still time and opportunity for them to live a useful, happy and blessed life. Mother-love, just like Jochebed's ark, is a careful weaving and intertwining of these readily available materials.

But the mother in our story did not stop here, either. She spent much time and effort preparing the ark to keep her child dry in the midst of the mighty Nile. She used the most reliable substance she knew to water-proof the vessel so that her child could be in the dangerous waters, yet remain untouched by them. You and I must follow her example before a child is launched into the world and world-proof the child's ark.

Try some old-fashioned rules and standards of conduct to world-proof your child's ark. Try some line-upon-line, precept-upon-precept Bible teaching that brings your little one early to Christ to world-proof your child's ark. Try some tearful, heart-searching prayer, some Scriptural ideals and principles incorporated into daily life, some heart-to-heart talks with genuine compassion about his childish cares to world-proof your child's ark.

Any mother with the same concern that Jochebed had can prayerfully seek out the right substances to prevent the world from leaking through to harm her precious child.

She Set Up a Watch.

When the little ark was launched with its precious

cargo, the mother set up a watch. Only after she had hidden her child away and prepared the vessel did she tenderly, and I am sure very tearfully, place him in those waters and set up a watch.

Even after our children are prayerfully launched into the world, it is still mother's place to set up a watch that prays effectually, advises wisely, and loves endlessly until death.

It is very true: "The hand that rocks the cradle rules the world." Although its importance is sometimes overlooked, in every generation there are some godly mothers who share Jochebed's realization of a mother's far-reaching influence.

"It is the mother who is a better citizen than the soldier who fights for his country. The successful mother, the mother...training aright the boys and girls who are to be the men and women of the next generation...occupies, if she only would realize it, a more honorable, more important position than any man in the community. The mother is the one supreme asset of the national life. She is more important, by far, than the successful statesman, or businessman, or artist, or scientist." (Theodore Roosevelt)

May God renew our understanding of the important calling on our lives as mothers, and may we renew our commitment to serve H im faithfully in the same. Only eternity will reveal the missions accomplished or the plan of God realized because of praying, loving mothers.

A Mom is like a Lighthouse,

Who brightens the darkest night
Who shows us the dangers lurking in
Our rough and stormy flight
And points us ever onward to safety and to home
A Mom's light shines the brightest when we feel all alone.

A Mom is like a medic team -- doctor, nurse, and orderly
Who prescribes and administers emergency care, watching carefully.
Whatever hurts and pains we feel,
We know she's always there,
And no matter the hurt, it's not half so bad
If you have a Mom to care.

A Mom is like the whole sports team,
The coach and cheerleader, too
She points out how we can do better
And encourages to start anew
When we're losing she's the diehard fan,
Who still knows we're the best,
And when the game is going our way
She's the one who's cheering loudest.

Mom is somewhat like the Bible, too;
Full of promises, warnings and commands.
She points us to right and honesty
And to always take a stand.
The wisdom and the love she gives
Are a lot like God's very own
And we know that all she ever wants
Is what's best for those at home.

She's kind of like rain and sunshine,
Necessary just to get by
Even if you could make it without her,
You wouldn't want to try.
So Mom, we tip our hats to you,
And send our thanks above
That God designed life complete with Mom,
To honor and to love.

-- Cathy Corle

12

Chapter Three

The Answer To A Mother's Problem

I read a story just yesterday of an efficiency expert, (which I'm sure I need) who addressed a ladies luncheon. He told them the most valuable thing they could learn to do is to meet their problems just one at a time and solve them. Repeatedly throughout his talk, he reiterated that point: "Don't try to take on all the problems of the world at once. Just meet them head on, one at a time, and you can solve anything." When he opened the session up for questions, one rather perplexed lady rose from her seat and asked, "Sir, I agree that we could solve our problems much more efficiently if we met them one at a time. But sir, please explain -- how are we supposed to get them to line up single file?"

Now I must confess, I needed that little laugh. But life does seem to be one set of problems after another. Everybody may not be dealing with the same types of problems - but you can be sure that everybody has got more than they know what to do with! Motherhood brings with

13

it a unique set of trials and victories, problems and solutions.

As I was considering the mothers in the Bible and how I might present their stories to mothers, this thought of problems and their solutions started clicking in my brain. I realized that each of these mothers had a problem, and that for every problem they had, God had the solution. They didn't need to get their solutions from the soap operas or Dr. Spock or secular psychologists or Oprah Winfrey or Dear Abbey or Ladies Hom e Journal, or any other worldly, humanistic source. They needed to get their solutions from the Lord. It's so important that we learn the same lesson, because our calling and ministry as mothers is so vital and important.

God could have taken that newborn babe
So innocent and helpless and sweet
And committed the care of that eternal soul
To an angel to cherish and keep.
The God of all power and inexhaustible love
Who puts each countless star where it goes
Who watches each sparrow lest it may fall
Could Himself train each child, if He chose.

He could even place us full-grown in the world
All ready to live on our own
But the God of creation Who made life's design
Knew the best way that it should be done.
So He took a woman and put into her heart
A bottomless barrel of love
And some of the tender compassion and warmth
That was in His own heart up above.

A yearning to give and a longing to care

The Answer To A Mother's Problem

God placed one by one in her heart
He made her ears able to hear during sleep
She was just about ready to start.
He put a prayer on her lips and a tear in her eye
And a comfort in her arms like no other,
Then God knew every child would have just what
he needs Because God had created a mother.
(Cathy Corle)

Hannah's Problem
A Desire Unfulfilled
(I Samuel 1:1-28)

The desire Hannah had was not wrong, it was a God-given desire. God has put the desire to be a mother in the heart of every little girl from the time that she's born. But for Hannah it was a desire unfulfilled, and it was a problem. She lived in a culture where polygamy was accepted, although it was never endorsed by God. Hannah had a problem because of the desire within and the enemy's taunting without. It's not hard to figure out that living in a household with two wives would present the prime opportunity to make enemies!

In this Old Testament culture, motherhood was still considered an honor, and to be childless was considered a disgrace. This was insult added to injury on top of a woman's heartcry to have a child to love and raise for the glory of God. She was shamed because of her inability to bear children. Humanism and ERA have tried to brainwash us against the natural, God-ordained desire and privilege of motherhood, but the Bible has not changed. It still says that motherhood is a woman's highest calling, and that ***"Children are an heritage of the Lord, and the fruit of the***

15

womb is his reward." (Psalm 127:3)

Notice what Hannah did about her problem.

1. **She prayed**. (v. 10) That is the right thing to do about every problem. God often lets us pray and wait for something He intends for us to have so we will realize its true value when we receive the answer to our prayers. How often do we seek the solution to a problem we face in every new book or magazine, and ask advice of every person we meet, but fail to bring it to God in prayer? It needs to be a deeply ingrained habit, that every problem, however big or small, would bring us to our knees before the Lord.

2. **She made a vow to God**. (v. 11) It is right to make holy, Bible-centered, Spirit-directed promises that we truly intend to keep. Too many people today are non-committal. "I don't want to promise..." But the truth is that they make promises about everything that is important to them. They have married, bought a house, signed an application promising to show up for work, and financed a car, and never said, "I don't like to make promises." Yet they won't go to an altar or raise their hands to volunteer when needed at church because they don't like to make promises. We are willing to make promises about things that we consider important, and there are times, often when we face a problem, that we need to make some holy vows to God.

3. **She shared her request with the man of God**. (v. 12-16) It's true that sharing a burden makes it seem only half as heavy. How often has it been such a release just to share with someone the request that seemed so weighty upon your heart? Your pastor and his wife are some of the most important people to share your requests with because they love you and pray for you, and they desire to see you grow spiritually. Their counsel is more apt to be God's counsel than your sister's or your neighbor's in most instances. They are the most likely people to pray for you and with you about any problem. Don't be afraid to share

your request with the man of God.

4. **She had faith that God would answer**. (v. 18) When Eli promised that God had heard her prayer and a baby would soon be on the way, she did not question him or wait for any further proof. She believed and went on her way joyfully, leaving the tears behind. We need to learn to pray in faith. Too many of us pray like those members of the early church praying for God to deliver Peter from prison. When Peter knocked on the door as a free man, they were terrified, thinking he was a ghost. How many times do we mouth a prayer that we really don't believe God can answer?

5. **She kept the vow that she had made.** We are quick to remind God of the promises He has made us when we face a problem. *"In the day of my trouble I will call upon thee: for thou wilt answer me."* *(Psalm 86:7)* But when God answers a prayer of distress, how easily we go on our way and forget the promises that we have made to Him. *"...I will pay thee my vows, Which my lips have uttered, and my mouth hath spoken, when I was in trouble."* *(Psalm 66:13-14)*

Hannah's promise was not an easy one to keep. She promised that if God would honor her desire with a son, that she would faithfully train him until he was weaned, and then she would be willing to part with him at that young age and leave him at the temple. There was no telephone system, and she could only visit with him once each year. We can only imagine what submission to the will of God that it required for Hannah to keep the promise she had made. We need to let Hannah serve as a reminder that in the calm we keep those holy vows that we made in the midst of the storm.

The Lord solved Hannah's problem and answered her prayers for a son. He used her faithful teaching, discipline, example and Bible training to prepare him for the role he was to fill in the spiritual guidance of a nation. During those few short years she had with Samuel, her godly influence far outweighed all the ungodly influence that Samuel was exposed to during his youth and teenage years. It's so important for us to realize the weight of our influence upon our children.

She's walking in my footsteps
That's very plain to see -
She says that when she's grown up
She wants to be just like me.
But it's a scary feeling,
Though one that brings me pride,
And it makes me pause and ponder
My heart, and what's inside.

Do I really want her
To be like me all the time?
Could I be proud to tell folks
That she's a child of mine?
Am I the kind of lady
That I want my girls to be?
Would it make me happy
If they DID turn out like me?

Or would it bring me heartbreak
If those wishes did come true-
"Mommy when I'm grown up
I want to be just like you"?
Would I have to shed some tears
And bow my head in shame
If what I am today
Is what my daughters soon became?

The Answer To A Mother's Problem

Dear Lord, I'm begging that You will
Remind me everyday
That little girls are watching
Everything I do and say
Lord, make me the kind of lady
Whose light the world can see
So I can be glad if my little girls
Grow up to be just like me.
(Cathy Corle 11-27-89)

Hannah's faithful, consistent, Biblical discipline during the first few years of Samuel's life overcame all the lack of discipline that reigned in his environment during all the remaining years. (Proverbs 23:13-14) ***"Withhold not correction from the child: for if thou beatest him with the rod, he shall not die. Thou shalt beat him with the rod, and shalt deliver his soul from hell."***

This is in contrast to the lack of discipline and control that Eli exercised with his sons. God told him he had made idols of them -- he put his children before God and honored their whims above the will of God. ***"For I have told him that I will judge his house for ever for the iniquity which he knoweth; because his sons made themselves vile, and he restrained them not."*** *(I Samuel 3:13)*

This mother, Hannah, learned through her problem and its solution the precious treasure that children are, and what a great blessing and privilege is ours when God entrusts a soul to our care. She learned the importance of example and discipline as a mother, and the urgent need to teach the Bible to our children. Hannah learned that when it comes to children, you should ***GET THEM FROM THE LORD.***

19

Mission: Motherhood
Eunice's Problem
A Divided Home

"Then came he to Derbe and Lystra: and, behold, a certain disciple was there, named Timotheus, the son of a certain woman, which was a Jewess, and believed; but his father was a Greek: Which was well reported of by the brethren that were at Lystra and Iconium. Him would Paul have to go forth with him;..." (Acts 16:1-3)

"When I call to remembrance the unfeigned faith that is in thee, which dwelt first in thy grandmother Lois, and thy mother Eunice; and I am persuaded in thee also." (II Timothy 1:5)

Eunice was a mother that had a problem. She was doing everything she could to raise her son for the glory of God, but her husband was an unbeliever, and their home was divided by the Gospel. How could she, alone, have the influence and control in a young man's life to train him so that he would be pure, Bible-centered, and equipped to be a great pastor in the days of the early church?

1. **She made the Bible pre-eminent** in her life, in her son's life and training, and in their home. She realized the absolute necessity of the power of the Scriptures to do what she could not do in her own power. Paul said to Timothy, *"And that from a child thou hast known the holy scriptures which are able to make thee wise unto salvation through faith which is in Christ Jesus." (II Timothy 3:14-15)*

Our promise of early salvation for our children hinges on whether or not we faithfully, consistently and lovingly present the Word of God to our children daily. It is the Bible in their hearts and minds that leads them to a childhood conversion. Reading, memorization, stories, games, quizzes, preaching... The Bible should be the center

The Answer To A Mother's Problem

of everything.

This mother knew the Bible was capable of doing a work in her son's life that she could not do herself. *"For the word of God is quick, and powerful, and sharper than any two-edged sword, piercing even to the dividing asunder of soul and spirit, and of the joints and marrow, and is a discerner of the thoughts and intents of the heart."* (Hebrews 4:12)

Her problem made her see the need, but we have just as great a need to instill the Scriptures in the hearts of our children, whether we see it or not. No matter what problem we face as mothers, the Bible has the answer, and often the Bible *is* the answer. Our children need the firm foundation of a life grounded in the Word of God.

2. **She welcomed the aid of other believing family members**. Timothy's grandmother, probably Eunice's mother, also taught him the Scriptures and trained him to be a godly young man. Grandparents can have a tremendous influence in the lives of their grandchildren for good or for wrong. Grandma, be sure that you are the right kind of example, that your home is a place where only good touches their lives, and let the time they spend with you bring them closer to the Saviour.

I'm a very important person,
I'm a Nana don't you see,
I have some darling little girls
that follow after me.
Even when I stumble on
the toys left here and there
They fill my heart with happiness,
and joy beyond compare.

Mission: Motherhood

With jam and jelly on their hands,
they fingerprint the door
And leave tiny little tracks
and footprints on the floor.
Sometimes they are quite noisy,
as they run about with glee
But it really doesn't matter,
I'm their Nana don't you see?

It's even fun to hold them,
and rock them on my lap
As they wiggle, punch and gouge me,
getting settled for a nap.
They have so much to tell me,
and they wait so patiently
Until I stop and listen,
I'm their Nana, don't you see?

Just when I think I'm settled,
they want to go bye-bye
They have a million potty calls
and could drink the ocean dry
Each day is full of mishap,
with their boo-boos and scraped knees
They need a lot of kisses
and much tender love from me.

I have a part in shaping
young lives for eternity.
I'm a very important person,
I'm a Nana, don't you see?
(Gladys Corle)

3. **She was willing to pay the price for her prayers to be answered.** God gave the solution to her problem when He opened the opportunity for Timothy to be under the influence and training of a man who was a godly example. But Eunice had to pay the price of separation when God opened the door and made His will clear. We read of no other children in the family, so quite possibly she was left alone. There were no telephones or postal services. She knew that travel was dangerous and quite possibly he might never return to her. BUT SHE HAD RAISED HIM FOR GOD -- NOT FOR HERSELF.

God had only one Son, and He willingly gave Him for us. How could we do less than give our children to Him? He loves them more than we do, He can care for them far beyond our power to do so. Have we raised our children for the glory of God, or do we raise them for ourselves? When we face a decision like this one, it will be clear which one of these is true.

I'm sure that there were many tearful prayers in the life of Eunice in behalf of her son Timothy, and God answered those prayers. God solved the problem of a divided home, and honored His word that was tenderly instilled into a child's heart. Eunice learned the importance of the Word of God in the salvation and training of children, and she learned that when it comes to children, you should *GIVE THEM TO THE LORD*

The Syrophenician's Problem
A Devil In Control

"Then Jesus went thence, and departed into the coasts of Tyre and Sidon. And, behold, a woman of Canaan came out of the same coasts, and cried unto him, saying, Have mercy on me, O Lord, thou Son of David; my daughter is grievously vexed with a devil. But he

answered her not a word. And his disciples came and besought him, saying, Send her away; for she crieth after us. But he answered and said, I am not sent but unto the lost sheep of the house of Israel. Then came she and worshipped him, saying, Lord, help me. But he answered and said, It is not meet to take the children's bread, and to cast it to dogs. And she said, Truth, Lord; yet the dogs eat of the crumbs which fall from their master's table. Then Jesus answered and said unto her, O woman, great is thy faith: be it unto thee even as thou wilt. And her daughter was made whole from that very hour." (Matthew 15:21-28)

This Syrophenician mother faced the problem of the devil's control in her child's life, a horrifying problem that needed the Lord's help. But she was separated by prejudice from the Jewish people and their Messiah. She was a descendent of Noah's grandson, Canaan, who brought a curse upon himself and all the generations born after him. She was actually living under the curse of God through no fault of her own. Most of the descendants of Canaan were destroyed when the children of Israel inherited the Promised Land, and there were just a few like herself, who were present during the time of Christ. We don't understand fully the impact of our sin being passed on to our children and their children, yet it is plainly taught in the Bible. How careful we ought to be!

She faced a problem of a devil who had sought and gained control in her precious child's life. The devil is seeking to influence and control our children as much as he did hers. He wants to send them to Hell. He wants to wreck their lives in sin and ruin before they ever get old enough to make adult decisions and face adult responsibilities. He wants to keep them from serving God and bringing others to Christ. He will use YOU to accomplish these things if you let him. He will take advantage of your unconcern and lack of action if you do not actively fight a spiritual warfare in behalf of your children.

The devil is seeking to influence and gain control in the lives of our children, and his tools are many. Humanism and atheism are a steady diet in the public schools and on television. The ungodly messages and beat in rock music erode their morals and leave their impress on little minds. Satanism and the occult are bombarding their minds from every source imaginable, the biggest being Saturday morning cartoons. TV and many other influences present sensual, sexual thoughts and desires to them everyday. The devil will use the wrong friends, the wrong heroes, and the wrong values to seek to destroy the little ones you love. What did she do with her problem?

1. **She recognized the problem for what it was -- Satan**. It was not just a harmless stage or a 'phase' she was going through that could afford to be ignored. It was not just a 'generation gap', an unimportant difference of opinion between children and parents. It was not just a matter of personal choice that did not have eternal consequences. THIS WAS A DANGEROUS, URGENT SITUATION THAT NEEDED CHRIST'S ATTENTION IMMEDIATELY!

2. **She realized that her child was beyond her own help** -- only God had the solution to this problem. Her child had to have the power of God to be delivered from the devil's control. It would not take care of itself or pass with time. It was a spiritual problem, not just mental or emotional. It was not for her to deal with a spiritual power much greater than herself. It could not be cared for by psychologists or secular counselors. ONLY GOD COULD HELP.

3. **She came to the Lord in behalf of her child's need.** How desperately our children need praying mothers who understand the need to solicit the Lord's deliverance for their children. Nothing can bring me to my knees more

quickly than a problem or a danger that concerns my children, and I believe there is a special place in the heart of God for a spirit-filled, interceding mother.

4. **She would not be discouraged or put off by the 'Christians' disdain and unconcern or by the Lord's 'SEEMING' unwillingness to meet her need.** Her child needed the Lord, and this mother was not about to let anything stand between herself and the solution. No price was too great. No distance was too far. No insult was too bitter. No miracle was too impossible. No humility was too lowly. Her child was in trouble, and a mother's love always comes to the rescue.

This Syrophenician mother brought her problem to the Lord, the problem of the devil's control. God solved her problem, answered her prayer and honored His Word. She learned the importance of a mother's earnest supplication and fighting a spiritual warfare in behalf of her child, and when it comes to your children, you must *GET THE LORD FOR THEM.*

The Unnamed Mothers' Problem A Dilemma Of Bringing Their Children To Christid

"Then were there brought unto him **little children..."** *(Matthew 19:13)* **"And they brought unto him also infants..."** *(Luke 18:15)* **"And they brought young children** *to him, that he should touch them: and his disciples rebuked those that brought them. But when Jesus saw it, he was much displeased, and said unto them, Suffer the little children to come unto me, and forbid them not: for of such is the kingdom of God. Verily I say unto you, Whosoever shall not receive the kingdom of God as a little child, he shall not enter therein. And he took them*

up in his arms, put his hands upon them, and blessed them." *(Mark 10:13-16)* These mothers faced a problem every mother faces. The dilemma of bringing your children to Jesus.

In Matthew 18 Jesus had just taught the people about child-like faith that is necessary for salvation. In essence, He said that children do not need to rationalize and understand like adults to be saved -- but adults need to have unquestioning faith like children in order to be saved. This was a brand new thing to their ears. Religion was mostly confined to adults, but salvation is for the little children.

After this teaching he traveled from Capernaum to Judea BUT it says that *'multitudes followed him'.* Very probably, these parents or at least some of them, had heard Jesus teach about children being saved, and their hearts had been stirred by Christ's expressions of love and concern and acceptance of little children.

This prompted them to know that if Jesus would accept little children, and bless their lives, then their children needed to be brought to Him right away. They faced opposition from other Christians, again, but Jesus would not let their lack of spiritual understanding put a barrier between the little ones and Himself. Jesus DOES love the little children, and we need to bring them to Him.

When they brought their children to Jesus: 1. He took them up in his arms -- protection and care. 2. He put his hands on them -- guidance and provision. 3. He blessed them -- A spiritual blessing that would go with them throughout their lives. We need to bring our children to Jesus in early childhood salvation -- it's our responsibility and our privilege. How can we bring our children to Christ?

1. Seek God's blessing upon them; dedicate them to God at birth.

2. Teach them **first** of Jesus and salvation which is more important than anything else we can teach them -- line

upon line -- day by day. Talk about salvation and how to get saved on a daily basis. *"And these words which I command thee this day, shall be in thine heart. And thou shalt teach them diligently unto thy children, and shalt talk of them when thou sittest in thine house, and when thou walkest by the way, and when thou liest down and when thou risest up." (Deuteronomy 6:6-7)* Make it part of everyday life.

3. Pray with them and for them regularly. Let them hear you pray for their salvation.

4. Hide God's Word in their hearts.

The Bible <<<   >>> Sin

Like opposite poles of a magnet, the Bible and sin repel one another. The surest way to fight sin and turn a child's heart away from evil is to fill them with the Bible. Remember God's promise of early salvation in II Timothy 3:15. The Scriptures make children *'wise unto salvation'*.

5. Keep them in an atmosphere of people being saved and baptized and bring their attention to it.

6. Keep them under a consistent diet of Bible preaching and teaching. Both of these are cared for just by keeping your entire family faithful in a strong, Bible preaching church. How many times have you seen people get out of church for some petty reason when their children were young and wanted to come, and then years later get right with God, but it was too late. Their children had grown up without God and the Bible. Our faithfulness is vital.

7. Watch for signs of conviction on their hearts and urge them to trust Christ.

Statistics say that 85% of all those who reach age 18 and have never trusted Christ to save them NEVER WILL. We can't take the chance of letting our children become one of those statistics and be separated from us forever in Hell. We must bring them to Jesus at an early age like these parents did.

28

The Answer To A Mother's Problem

"It is easiest to lead a child from 5 to 10 years to a definite acceptance of Christ. I rejoice in the work done by rescue missions, where we see the wrecks of manhood and womanhood changed into noble men and women. But this is not the work that produces the most satisfactory Christians. The younger we get a child to accept Christ and begin Christian training, the more beautiful the product. The overwhelming majority in our church were converted before 21 years of age. Whatever your church does, let it do its full duty by the children." *(R. A. Torrey)*

There are little feet that follow you
wherever you may please
They struggle hard to match the steps
that come to you with ease.
The thoughtless journeys that we take
in carelessness each day
Are watched by thoughtful admiring eyes
that follow close the way.

Where do the steps lead you have left
for little feet to trod?
Do they wander paths of sin,
or do they walk with God?
Do they wander to and fro
from one whim to another?
Or do they leave example plain
of love to every brother?

Will your footsteps guide those feet
through confusion and desperation?
Or will they lead him straight to God
and Christ's blood-bought salvation?

Mission: Motherhood

Will he follow you to walk
in worldly wisdom still?
Or can he follow step-by-step
within God's perfect will?

When your little one is all grown up
it may be too late to do
To change the example you have left,
for he wants to be 'just like you'.
Those little feet will follow you
to walk with God or stray --
You determine his path for tomorrow
by the steps you take today.
(Cathy Corle)

"I have no greater joy than to hear that my children walk in truth." (II J ohn 4) John is talking about his spiritual children, those he won to the Lord. The greatest joy of his life was to see them growing and maturing in the Lord. We know what a great joy it is to our hearts to watch our children grow up, and rejoice with every new accomplishment and ability they acquire.

There is a special bond between a new convert and the soulwinner who brought him to Christ. There is also a special bond between a child and the parents who brought him into the world. It is our wonderful joy to be able to share BOTH of those relationships with our children. We can bring them into the world and love and care for them. We can be the instrument of bringing them to Jesus and seeing them grow in the Christian life.

These mothers learned that the Lord can solve the problems of bringing our children to a definite acceptance of eternal salvation, and that when it comes to children you should **GET THEM TO THE LORD.** Don't miss the incomparable joy of bringing your little ones to Jesus.

There are many other mothers, and many problems that they faced, but it may suffice to say, mother, that the Lord has the solution to every problem. He IS the solution to every problem. He allows these problems to teach us some things, and to help us to realize the precious eternal value of our children, and to keep us leaning on Him.

GET THEM FROM THE LORD
In prayer dedicate your child and yourself to God.

GIVE THEM TO THE LORD
Let the Lord use you to prepare their lives, then let the Lord use them in His service.

GET THE LORD FOR THEM
Be ready for the spiritual warfare and pray earnestly and with tears for the Lord to win the battle over the devil in your child's life.

GET THEM TO THE LORD
Claim God's promise for the early salvation of your children and YOU be the one who gets them saved.

Mary answered the Call to Motherhood with Submission to God's Will:

"...Behold the handmaid of the Lord; be it unto me according to thy word..."
Luke 1:38

Chapter Four

A Praying Mother

The dictionary definition of mother just says, "The female parent of a child" --- however, any mother could tell you that there's much more to it than that. In fact, just about anybody of any age would say that the word 'Mother' means much more than what that definition portrays. Poems and songs and books and essays have been composed through the ages by people who tried to express what 'Mother' means to them.

If motherhood came in a can where we could read the ingredients on the label, it might sound something like this.

No one knows the exact ingredients
Of which its formulated
But it stands among the mightiest of
Wondrous works that God's created
It's love beyond understanding,
And on earth there is no other
That can compare unto the love

33

Mission: Motherhood
Within the heart of Mother.

Patience and understanding,
Encouragement and smiles
Compassion, hope and confidence
That are felt across the miles
Forgiveness and 'forgetness'
Sweet beyond all measure
Are all a part of what's in her heart –
A love her child will treasure.

It's a pain in her heart
When her child cries–
It's a fear when he faces danger
It's a constant prayer for the yet-to-be,
To intercession she's no stranger.
It's disappointment drowned in forgiveness,
And dishwater mingled with tears.
It's the sleep that listens for a child's cry
That only a mother hears.

It's hundreds of trips to the doctor,
And thousands of home-cooked meals
It's countless sleepless nights beside
A child with fever and chills.
It's piano lessons and ball games,
And school plays by the score,

A Praying Mother

For which Mom, (of course!)
is always chauffeur,
And still it's much, much more.

All the diapers and laundry and dishes,
And fingerprints on the glass
All the muddy footprints tracked across
The floor that's just been waxed.
All the frogs and worms
In sock drawers,
And the stains that won't come out
All the bruises and scraped up knees
That Mom knows all about.

All the silent tears and heartcries
Are counted one by one;
And the Lord will not forget them
When its time to hear, "Well Done."
Probably a thousand other things
Known only to God above
Should be part of the list of ingredients
That make up a Mother's Love.
(Cathy Corle)

There was once a day when I knew everything there was to know about 'How To Be The Perfect Mom'. I mean, I had read all the books, listened to all the tapes -- I knew it all. I knew what everyone else did wrong, that of course, I would do right. I knew all the pat answers and how-to-do-it formulas and secrets for perfect children. I was an expert on motherhood until something happened that messed everything up. You're right -- I had children! That put an end to all my expertise.

Motherhood IS our most important project or goal or calling in life. Making a million dollars or working your way up the corporate ladder cannot even compare to the important job we have for which we wear the title 'MOM'. We may do many other things, but nothing as eternal OR as irreversible as rearing our children. What an awesome responsibility God has placed in our hands to mold and shape little lives for the future.

Stop and think about what we do...When we start out on something important that we want to do well, we have high hopes and great expectations. We're just sure that we're going to impress everyone, we're going to do such a startling great job at reaching our goal. We start out on something with 'PLAN A', sure that everything will follow our wishes. And it does, at least for five minutes. Then something goes wrong and 'PLAN A' goes up in a puff of smoke.

So we say, "OK, I'm flexible. Let's design a 'PLAN B'. So we come up with Plan B and make allowance for the monster that killed 'PLAN A'. We're so proud of our flexibility and ingenuity as we set out toward our goal with 'PLAN B' in hand. Then something else goes wrong.

So we let out a sigh, grit our teeth, scratch our head and start those gears grinding. We think of every possible thing that COULD possibly go wrong and plan for it. Then somewhat disillusioned, but nonetheless determined, we set out for victory with 'PLAN C'. But something happens that we hadn't thought of.

When we've exhausted our patience, our ingenuity and

36

the whole alphabet, and 'PLAN Z' has fallen flat on its face, then we finally fall on our faces and say, "Oh, God! I thought I could do this for you. I wanted to do it so well. I wanted to be a success. I wanted to have victory. But Lord, I'm finding out that I just can't do anything. Here I am with this important job to do and I can't do it. I thought I was so capable, and now I'm learning that I'm helpless. Lord, if You need this job done, You're going to have to do it. I can't do anything without you. But I believe You can do it, and I believe you can do it through me. Lord, I'm at the bottom in defeat. Please help me." And God says, "Now I can do what I've been wanting to do all along."

Tell me -- why don't we start out that way? Why don't we embark on our important task by realizing before we start that we can't do it without the Lord's power and strength and wisdom and love and patience? Why do we wait until we've messed things up so badly before we ask Him for the help that He's been longing to give us?

In John 15:5 Jesus said very plainly: ***"Without me ye can do NOTHING."*** I mean, how much more specific can you get? But He didn't leave us hopeless. In Philippians 4:13 I read this promise: ***"I can do ALL THINGS through Christ which strengtheneth me."*** Why do we wait so long to learn that?

Being a mom is a lot more important than building a monument or writing a book or making a fortune. Why don't we start out with prayer instead of waiting until we fall flat on our faces? Why don't we begin by crying out to God, by admitting our own inability and drawing on God's strength and wisdom and patience and love? Wouldn't we save ourselves a lot of heartache?

When they place that new baby in our arms, why don't we throw away all our pat answers and fancy formulas and say, "OH GOD -- I can't raise this child to be what you want him or her to be. Dear God, I'm nothing but a wretched hell-deserving sinner saved by the grace of God. There's nothing in me that can be the kind of mother that will mould and train and bend and shape an **eternal person** to fit your **eternal purpose.** But God -- I know You can. I'm asking You to raise and mother this child THROUGH me. I'm asking for the Holy Spirit to fill me and work through me to do this most important job that I cannot do on my own."

Maybe I'm talking to a new mother with high hopes, and wonderful dreams for that new bundle of joy at your house. Just a friendly word of advice. Please don't learn the hard way. No matter how much you love that child or how good your intentions and resolve to be a perfect mom, without God you can do nothing.

Maybe I'm talking to a burdened, disillusioned mother at the other end of the spectrum with shattered dreams and broken hopes -- a mother whose children have broken her heart, and she has given up all hope of raising her children to serve the Lord and live godly, fruitful lives. Here's the encouragement you need: "You can do all things THROUGH Christ."

"Nothing lies beyond the reach of prayer except that which lies beyond the will of God." No matter how far your child may have wandered into sin, don't give up. Never stop praying. If Mom doesn't pray for them and love them, who will? If that one is still living on this earth, then God hasn't given up on them, and all hope is not lost. Don't you give up on them either, Mom.

Prayer is not just the last resort. For mothers prayer should be the first thought, the initial step, the last breath, the final thanksgiving and everything in between. Oh how we need mothers today who will learn to pray and pray with all their might. Our children need praying mothers.

I no longer feel like an expert on motherhood. Now I

can see myself as a helpless, hopeless, completely dependent child of God who needs His power to do His work. I know that if my children turn out right, it won't be because I'm a great mother, but because I have a great God -- a prayer hearing, prayer answering God that gave me these children, that loves them even more than I do, that is even more concerned about how their lives turn out than I am.

I feel keenly the need to pray and turn things over to God. I've learned that on my own I only make a mess of things, but when God's Hands take over, then something beautiful and eternal is the result. Oh how I need to pray for my children.

PRAYER AND PREPARATION

Before you ever hold that baby in your arms, determine in your heart that motherhood is a high calling and privilege and that you want to let God work through you to raise that child for His glory. Read some good books and memorize some verses and make some decisions about how you will raise your children. Before they have children, or even before they marry, a couple can pray together and promise the Lord and one another that they will obey the Scriptures and raise their children in the nurture and admonition of the Lord.

An expectant mom ought to pray everyday for that child and ask for God's best. Elisabeth prayed and praised God for her unborn son, and John the Baptist was filled with the Holy Spirit even before he was born.

Before a child is even born ought to be a time of prayer and preparation. What kind of preparation? First of all, keep the Bible first of all. Pay close attention to what God has to say about child-training. List and memorize some verses that deal with child-training and discipline. All the formulas in the world won't replace the promises and principles contained in the Word of God, the handbook for Life.

Read some other good books like J. Richard Fugate's book, "What The Bible Says About Childtraining." Listen to good preaching and listen to what your pastor has to say. But be careful that you don't get overbalanced on the subjects of marriage and children at the expense of soulwinning and serving God in other areas.

I know that this is not profound -- it may even sound unnecessary. But most of us need to be reminded that you can't be a good wife and mother without being a good Christian. God meant for us to do both, and we cannot train our children to obey Him while we disobey Him.

One of the most valuable avenues of preparation is to watch good examples -- folks who you admire in their relationship to their children, folks who are living out the Biblical principles that you are learning. Through our years on the road I have had the privilege of seeing so many good, godly homes first-hand, and seeing how you turn those verses into shoe-leather. What an encouragement it is to see a family whose children have the kind of attitude and testimony that I pray mine will have at that age, and to see their relationship with their parents.

The preparation stage of motherhood is so important. We have more of the world's philosophy and the humanistic mind-set than we dare to imagine, so it's important that we ON PURPOSE look into the Word of God and pray in preparation for motherhood. START OUT IN PREPARATION -- BUT DON'T FORGET TO PRAY.

A Praying Mother
PRAYER AND PRACTICE

God could have taken that newborn babe
So innocent and helpless and sweet
And committed the care of that eternal soul
To an angel to cherish and keep.
The God of all power and inexhaustible love
Who puts each countless star where it goes
Who watches each sparrow lest it may fall
Could Himself train each child, if He chose.

He could even place us full-grown in the world
All ready to live on our own
But the God of creation Who made life's design
Knew the best way that it should be done.
So He took a woman and put into her heart
A bottomless barrel of love
And some of the tender compassion and warmth
That was in His own heart up above.

A yearning to give and a longing to care
God placed one by one in her heart
He made her ears able to hear during sleep --
She was just about ready to start.
He put a prayer on her lips and a tear in her eye
And a comfort in her arms like no other,
Then God knew every child would have
just what he needs
Because God had created a mother.

Mission: Motherhood

Now we're down to the nitty-gritty. We saw how 'PLAN A' and 'PLAN B' looked so wonderful, but kids don't always fall into our well-laid plans. It's important to prepare, but when we start putting our plans into practice, we're going to discover the need to pray.

Someone said a principle or conviction is a decision made in advance. We need to have some Scriptural principles and convictions concerning how we raise our children and then stick to them no matter how hard it gets. Like: "When my child willfully disobeys me, this is how I will respond..."

It's hard at 2 a.m. when you haven't had a full night's sleep in weeks. When you've spanked a child 4 or 5 times already and he still defies you, it's hard to stick to your resolve. I can remember the terrible two's that seemed to last 20 years. Usually I broke their will. Sometimes they broke my will. But practice what you know is right no matter how hard it gets.

If you don't have some decisions made in advance about how you will do things, you'll find yourself vacillating constantly instead of being consistent. Then once those principles have been carefully decided, just do what you've decided to do, no matter how hard it gets. It doesn't matter how great your plans and dreams and preparation have been -- none of it will come to pass if you don't put it into practice.

"Train up a child in the way he should go, and when he is old he will not depart from it." (Proverbs 22:6) That's the verse we've been claiming for years, isn't it? But the promise doesn't apply to ANY way I choose for him to go -- but THE way God has chosen and outlined in the Bible.

Andrew Murray was a missionary with 10 children, definitely not an easy undertaking in anyone's estimation.

A Praying Mother

All 10 of his children grew up to be full time servants of the Lord as well as pure, godly Christians. He said this, "TRAIN is a word of deep importance for every parent to understand. Training is not telling, not teaching, not commanding, but something higher than all of these. It is not only *telling a child what to do*, but also *showing him how to do it* and then *seeing that it is done*."

Put those convictions and principles into practice and be consistent in everyday life, but don't forget to pray.

PRAYER AND PROBLEM SOLVING
(I Kings 4:1-7)

"Now there cried a certain woman of the wives of the sons of the prophets unto Elisha, saying, Thy servant my husband is dead; and thou knowest that thy servant did fear the LORD: and the creditor is come to take unto him my two sons to be bondmen. And Elisha said unto her, What shall I do for thee? tell me, what hast thou in the house? And she said, Thine handmaid hath not any thing in the house, save a pot of oil.
Then he said, Go, borrow thee vessels abroad of all thy neighbours, even empty vessels; borrow not a few. And when thou art come in, thou shalt shut the door upon thee and upon thy sons, and shalt pour out into all those vessels, and thou shalt set aside that which is full.
So she went from him, and shut the door upon her and upon her sons, who brought the vessels to her; and she poured out. And it came to pass, when the vessels were full, that she said unto her son, Bring me yet a vessel. And he said unto her, There is not a vessel more. And the oil stayed. Then she came and told the man of God. And he said, Go, sell the oil, and pay thy debt, and live thou and thy children of the rest."

Here was a mother in the Old Testament who was

showered upon with more grief and heartache than most of us ever imagine. H er husband had been studying and preparing for ministry under the prophet, Elisha. Already in poverty, nursing a dying husband, now her husband was gone and someone to whom he owed money had come to collect from her. In that day it was possible for a creditor to take the children of a debtor to be indentured servants, and use their labor to pay off debts. This was the situation. She had only a short time to find an answer to her problem.

I want you to notice the steps that she took in problem-solving. She went to the man of God. Go to your preacher. Are you practicing what he preaches? He loves you. He knows you. He prays for you. Don't go to the psychiatrist and the counselor and the humanistic magazines and books and philosophies. Go to the man of God who will give you God's answer to your problem. She had the faith to take the advice the man of God gave, even though it probably didn't sound like a workable solution when she heard it.

Notice also that God used what she had -- an ordinary little container with a small amount of oil. God used what she had. She didn't have much, but God saw to it that she had all she needed.

She had faith to dream big. He said, "Borrow not a few," so she got as many vessels as she could get her hands on. There is no limit on God's power. She not only could sell the oil for enough to pay the debt, but lived on the remaining sum -- no longer in such deep poverty. Sometimes God uses a crisis like this to teach us to trust Him and to give us more and better than we had before the problem arose.

Learn to come to God with every problem. If you're a mother, there will be problems along the way. LET JESUS SOLVE YOUR PROBLEM -- BUT DON'T FORGET TO PRAY.

A Praying Mother
PRAYER AND PRAISE

God's promises are true. If we set out with prayer and raise our children with daily prayer, see that they are saved and surrendered, and pray through the problems that we encounter, we will surely have the privilege of praise in a few years. God will honor our prayers and we will be able to look back and thank God for every prayer, every tear and every step of the way.

I'm convinced that a praying mother is the best mother any child could possibly have. What kind of a mother will she be?

God-fearing	Christ-honoring
Spirit-filled	Bible-centered
A good example	Loving
Kind	Patient
Observant	Teaching

A good and loving wife (The biggest favor you can do your children is love their daddy.)

No matter what books you read or what seminars you go to, they're going to tell you that these are the important things in motherhood. God said, "If you just pray daily and fervently, I want to make you a good mother."

I'm convinced that America's only hope is in praying mothers. How would praying Godly mothers affect the course of this nation? "The future destiny of a child is the life's work of a mother. Let France have good mothers and she will have good sons." --Napoleon Bonaparte

"When all is said, it is the mother, and the mother only, who is a better citizen than the soldier who fights for his country. The successful mother, the mother who does her part in rearing and training aright the boys and girls who are to be the men and women of the next generation, is of greater use to the community, and occupies, if she only would realize it, a more honorable as well as a more important position than any man it it. The mother is the one supreme asset of the national life. She is more important, by far, than the successful statesman, or businessman, or artist, or scientist." --Theodore Roosevelt

I am trusting the Lord that my children are going to turn out right - and when they do, God will get all the glory. I've proven over and over again that I'm no expert on motherhood. I don't expect my name to go down in history, or my likeness to appear in some motherhood hall of fame.

But I do want my children to know that I pray for them, and I do want Heaven to hear me call out their names in prayer on a daily basis. I do want to bombard Heaven with my petition so much that God would be embarrassed to let my kids be a disgrace to Him because He knows and they know and everyone else knows how much I've prayed for them.

The more I read the Bible and look at myself, I see my weaknesses and failures very clearly. No I'll never be an expert on motherhood -- but I wouldn't mind being called a praying mom.

Billy Sunday credited his conversion and ministry to his mother's prayers. Joe Boyd came back to God and preached because of his mother's prayers. Jack Hyles came home triumphant from facing the biggest time of temptation during his teenage years to find his mother on her knees, praying for him. I'm realizing more every day that no mother is really a good mother unless she is a praying mother.

Yes, when you get to the end of your rope --- pray. (And if you're a mother, you WILL get to the end of your rope now and then.) But don't wait till you get to the end of your rope before you pray. Begin with prayer, continue with prayer, overcome difficulties with prayer, and crown your success when your children are grown and serving God with prayer of thanksgiving, and a continual holding them before the throne of grace for as long as you bear the name "Mother". Don't wait until problems arise and your children are half grown to learn to pray for them. Start today, wherever you are in this time-line as a mother.

Someone asked a mother whose children had turned out very well, the secret by which she had prepared them for the future. Without hesitation she replied: "When in the morning I washed my children, I prayed that they might be cleansed by the Saviour's precious Blood. When I dressed them for the day, I prayed that they might be arrayed in the garments of salvation and in the robe of Christ's righteousness. When I prepared their meals, I prayed that they might be fed with the Bread of Life. When I started them on the road to school, I prayed that their faith might be as a shining light to lead them throughout their lives. When I rocked them to sleep each night, I prayed that they might be enfolded in the arms of the everlasting God. I guess if there is any secret to what I may have done for my children, it was prayer." What a joy to that mother's heart when her children arise up and call her blessed.

There is no greater gift or service that we can do for our children, no legacy more valuable, no methodology more fool-proof in training them for God's glory than to be a praying mother.

Mission: Motherhood

There's a picture I remember
Although I'm growing old
It's the picture of my mother
As her hands in prayer she'd fold.
She prayed each day at even tide
For health and clothes and food
And we never did without a thing,
Her prayers God understood.

She'd sit beside our bed of pain
And pray the whole night long
Our pain was gone with morning light,
From the kitchen came her song.
This was her way to thank the Lord
For answering her prayers,
She sing, "Jesus Took My Burden"
As she softly climbed the stairs.

Now, sometimes, my day has problems
That I do not understand
But then in fond remembrance
I see Mother's Praying Hands.
Then I fold mine too, in reverence,
And in secret softly pray
For the God Who answered Mother's prayers
To answer mine today.

Oh, yes the memories of Mother
Through the years I will recall,
But the memory of her Praying Hands
I remember best of all.
(Selected)

Chapter Five

A Closer Look at the Ministry of MOM

Motherhood is our most important project or goal or calling in life. Making a million dollars or working your way up the corporate ladder cannot even compare to the important job we have for which we wear the title 'MOM'. No job, no title, no paycheck, no benefit package in the world can outdo the advantages of this rewarding career. We may do many other things, but nothing as eternal OR as irreversible as rearing our children. What an awesome responsibility God has placed in our hands to mold and shape lives for the future.

Yes, it is a big responsibility, and that's why you've got some women running the other way in this irresponsible, here-for-the-fun generation. But every blessing has an equal responsibility, and vice-versa. Why is it someone would be glad to take care of the maintenance on a $500,000 home with a picture perfect lawn? They must agree that the blessing is equal to the responsibility or commitment required. Well, I'm not the only mother that will tell you that the blessings in store for you in the role of mom are well worth the responsibilities entailed. Kisses and hugs and dandelion bouquets and construction paper cards are merely the tip of the iceberg!

Stop and consider that motherhood is not just a part of God's plan for some -- it IS God's plan for me as a lady. God made the first woman in the world with the ability and the command to have children and raise them for Him. Even when given her name, her identity, Adam said, *"She shall be called Eve, because she is the mother of all living."* Most all of the women used of God in the Bible were used and blessed in their role as wife and mother, such as Mary, Hannah, Eunice, Manoah's wife, and many others. You can't separate motherhood from your identity or your calling once that first little flannel-wrapped bundle arrives.

I'm afraid that we've gotten away from acknowledging the honor of motherhood, the high value and privilege, and the important work that it is. Let me rephrase that -- as a mother of teenagers, I'm afraid maybe I'VE gotten away from it. While many girls feel a definite burden and desire to prepare as a Christian school teacher, a missionary, a secretary, or some other outside responsibility, I think we need to remind them that the most important part of a lady's work of serving the Lord is in the home. For those young ladies who don't plan to do any of those things, we need to let them know that they still have a responsibility to serve God in the most important task He made them for. They still have something important and exciting to prepare for. Let's get back to honoring the high call of motherhood, and treating it as the important and rewarding job that it is.

Remember that the family is set up to give the world a picture of God, and God designed the family members so that they picture the Trinity. There is only one God, but with three distinct personalities, positions, jobs and responsibilities. Inside one family unit, we see the same diversity. It's easy to see that the Father is the member of the family who pictures God the Father, and the children are in the place that coincides with God the Son. If that be so, then who is it at your house and mine that is in the place of the Holy Spirit? That's right, it's nobody else but Mom.

Most churches have a 'do-every-thing-guy'. When my husband first surrendered to preach, before he went to Bible College, he served the Lord in a local church. He was the bus director, a bus captain, the bus mechanic, working in the youth department and picking up teens for activities, supervisor in the Christian school, and any other job that no one else would do. I've learned that many men of God have spent a time in their early ministry and training filling a place like this.

Mom is that kind of jack-of-all-trades, the wearer of many hats, the doer of many jobs. There is only one person in the game of life who can be trainer, coach, referee, teammate, emergency medical squad, cheerleader and pep rally promoter all at the same time. That's MOM. She's also nurse, counselor, comforter, teacher, disciplinarian, veterinarian, band-aid dispenser, and boo-boo kisser. To get a good look at some of the responsibilities a mom ought to be taking care of, look at all the ministries of the Holy Spirit. I have gotten a blessing from looking at the different ministries of the Holy Spirit and comparing them with my life as a mom.

Study also about God's attributes as parent-father toward his children. For example: Giving. "For God so loved the world that He ____" What? Gave! We tend to think of giving to our children as spoiling them only. But I think it also has to do with the fact that we're made in the image of God, and we've inherited His deep desire to give good things to His children. *"Every good gift and every perfect gift is from above and cometh down from the Father of lights, with whom is no variableness, neither shadow of turning."* (James 1:17) It's God's character remade in us to love and give to our children. Now, I realize that it can get out of balance with our sinful natures and our bent toward materialism at the exclusion of their more important needs, but we all have an innate desire to give our children what we had and more than we had. I don't think that desire is always wrong, it's just another natural desire that has to be controlled.

As you read Romans 8, you again see that God wants His children to have everything we need and want. He wants to answer our prayers and fill our requests, but it hinges on our obedience and conformity to His will. He first predestinated or planned for us to be conformed to the image of His son in verse 29. With that in progress, He made this promise. *"He that spared not his own Son, but delivered him up for us all, how shall he not with him also freely give us all things?"* (Romans 8:32) How does our Heavenly Father desire to give to us? Freely. How much does He want to provide for us? All things! It sounds like He wants to spoil me if I would just let Him!

I remember when my girls first entered the stage where they've planned their weddings 4,000 different ways with Mr. Mystery always waiting at the altar. (Who cares who the maid of honor is if you don't even know who the groom is yet?) The colors, the dresses, the cake, the decorations, and where they'd like to spend their honeymoon have been planned and replanned over and over again. But that's such a natural part of the teenage years, and looking forward to what and who the Lord has for you is part of the fun. Even before they reached the age where they're permitted to date, I told them that the kind of wedding they can afford has a lot to do with them doing right between there and the altar.

A Closer Look at the Ministry of Mom

I wanted to see them date with godly standards and a submissive attitude toward parents and rules, and prayerfully be sure they marry the man of God's choosing, and do things right. I determined that if they would do their part, I'll probably turn my pockets inside out to try to make their dreams come true. You know what? I have a feeling that's how God feels about us. He promised in Psalm 84:11, *"No good thing will he withhold from them that walk uprightly."*

I want to look at some of the ministries of the Holy Spirit, and remind myself as I remind you about how that relates to our ministry as a mom. We've already introduced mom as the Holy Spirit of the home, and now I'd like for you to take a look with me at some of the ministries of the Holy Spirit, which coincide with some of the jobs and responsibilities that mom can care for in the lives of her children.

SECURITY AND ASSURANCE

In the heart of every child of God, it is the ministry of the Holy Spirit to confirm our place of belonging and value in God's family and in His Home in Heaven. Consider these verses from I John. *"Hereby know we that we dwell in him, and he in us, because he hath given us of his Spirit."* (I John 4:13) *"...And hereby we know that he abideth in us, by the Spirit which he hath given us."* (I John 3:24) *"...And it is the Spirit that beareth witness, because the Spirit is truth."* (I John 5:6) *"He that believeth on the Son of God hath the witness in himself:.."* (I John 5:10) Romans chapter eight also teaches that this is one of the important ministries of the Holy Spirit to every believer. *"The Spirit itself beareth witness with our spirit, that we are the children of God."* (Romans 8:16)

Mission: Motherhood

As a young preacher's wife, I battled for a time with security, and it drove me to the Scriptures to look for answers. One of the most important things that I learned is that it is very possible for a person who is genuinely saved to lack security in their hearts and minds. Because it is the job of the precious H oly Spirit to provide assurance, whenever we have grieved or quenched the Spirit, whenever we have allowed sin and bitterness and hard-heartedness to rule and reign, then we are missing out on this assuring, security-providing service that the Holy Ghost provides.

Mom is the Holy Spirit of the home, and this is also a job for her to do. Though not many of our children need assurance that they are truly part of the family and welcome in the home, they do need security and assurance and peace of mind through the ministry of mom. A mother's love gives assurance of worth, of place or position or belonging in the family and in life. Our children need to be assured of our love and unconditional acceptance. They need mom to believe in who they are and who God made them to be, especially during those times when they have a hard time believing in themselves. God designed loving families with parents and grandparents, so that every child could have one haven to run to where he or she is the best, the brightest, the greatest and the most important person in the world. I need to provide my children with assurance and security and belonging.

CONVICTION AND CHASTENING

Mom, like the Holy Spirit, can team up with a guilty conscience when it comes to dealing with sin and disobedience in a child's life. Discipline is an act of love, not an act of anger or punishment. True Bible discipline says, "I love you too much to let you do wrong and have the heartache and unhappiness that sin brings. I love you so much that I don't want you to pay the high cost of the wages of sin."

The Bible says repeatedly that it is LOVE that is behind chastening and correction. *"...My son, despise not thou the chastening of the Lord, nor faint when thou art rebuked of him: For whom the Lord loveth he chasteneth, and scourgeth every son whom he receiveth. If ye endure chastening, God dealeth with you as with sons; for what son is he whom the father chasteneth not?"* *(Hebrews 12:5-7)* *"He that spareth his rod hateth his son: but he that loveth him chasteneth him betimes."* *(Proverbs 13:24)* *"My son, despise not the chastening of the Lord; neither be weary of his correction: For whom the Lord LOVETH he correcteth; even as a father the son in whom he delighteth."* *(Proverbs 3:11-12)* *"Correct thy son, and he shall give thee rest; yea, he shall give delight unto thy soul."* *(Proverbs 29:17)* *"The rod and reproof give wisdom: but a child left to himself bringeth his mother to shame."* *(Proverbs 29:15)*

Conviction is another facet. *"Nevertheless I tell you the truth; It is expedient for you that I go away: For if I go not away, the Comforter will not come unto you; but if I depart, I will send him unto you. And when he is come, he will reprove the world of sin, and of righteousness, and of judgment:"* *(John 16:7-8)* As Holy Spirit at home, it's our job to bring sin to the light of God's Word, to admonish and rebuke wrong-doing, and to administer correction and chastening.

Remember that, as part of the God-head, the Holy Spirit is omniscient, or all-knowing. (Remember that old commercial: "It's 11:00 p.m. Do you know where your children are?") I had a wonderful teacher in this respect.

55

Mission: Motherhood

My mom could always find out what I was up to. When I was very little, if I was sneaking around doing something I was told not to do, I always got hurt or had some sort of accident and she found out. In high school, I told all my friends that she read my Bible (and all the notes and demerit slips and whatever else I filed between the pages during the day), she sometimes peeked into my notebooks from school, especially the scrawl along the edges where I was daydreaming instead of taking notes, and she also showed interest in my trash can any time I had been spring-cleaning in my bedroom. I was not often encouraged to spend the night at my friends' homes, yet they were always welcome at our house, and my parents usually put up with a houseful or yard-full of kids. She made it her business to know where I was and what I was up to and who I was with. The one time in all my school years that I skipped the last class of the day and went to the park, my mom found out about it after I graduated! She was the self-appointed private investigator, yet she always had a fun attitude and genuine interest in what was going on in my life. I thank the Lord for my 'nosy mom', and that my parents were concerned enough to watch out for me the best they knew how as I grew up.

Proverbs 31 teaches us that *'she looketh well to the ways of her household.'* I've heard people say that this meant her housekeeping and management skills, yet I believe it refers more to the people of her household, just as it does when it says, *'all her household are clothed in scarlet.'* The word that is translated 'looketh well' means 'to study, to lean toward and peer into, to examine carefully'. I think it's my job as a mom to 'look well' to the ways of all those in my family. I should be closely involved enough to know what's going on, what attitudes prevail, who needs encouragement or reprimand, and what's

A Closer Look at the Ministry of Mom

foremost in each person's heart and mind. Sometimes my children need encouragement, but other times they need a reminder or a rebuke. It just depends on what's going on in their lives right now. That takes time and closeness and involvement. When a mother has this kind of ministry in her children's lives, then she's the first one to know when the need arises for dealing with sin and disobedience, and she's close enough to her children to know what is the best way to deal with it.

TEACHER AND REMINDER

"But the Comforter, which is the Holy Ghost, whom the Father will send in my name, he shall teach you all things and bring all things to your remembrance, whatsoever I have said unto you." (John 14:26) Much of Bible preaching and teaching is not in revealing new truth, but in repeating and reminding us of what we've already learned. Just as we need to constantly be reminded and retaught about the same subjects of prayer, Bible reading, soulwinning, tithing, etc, we need to realize that our children also require line-upon-line repetition of the basic things that are most important. It's our job to teach our children about God and the Bible, about sin and salvation, about morality and dating and marriage and family, about character and God's commands for us and plan for our lives.

The Bible tells us that teaching the Bible to our children should be a constant, repetitive process in Deuteronomy 6:5-7. *"And thou shalt love the Lord thy God with all thine heart, and with all thy soul, and with all thy might. And these words, which I command thee this day, shall be in thine heart: And thou shalt teach them diligently unto thy children, and shalt talk of them when thou sittest in thine house, and when thou walkest by the way, and when*

57

thou liest down, and when thou risest up."

Sometimes I feel like all I get done as a mother is reminding. "Have you read your Bible?" "Did you wash the dishes?" "Did you mow the lawn?" "Did you clean your room?" "Have you finished your schoolwork?" But we also need to be reminding them of important topics like honesty and integrity, diligence, compassion, and testimony to the world.

Mom, you are the number one teacher in your child's life. You're the one who comes first. You're the one who's still there when they graduate and move on. You are the most important and influential teacher your child will ever have. They not only learn from what you say, but also from what you do. "When all is said and done, more is caught than taught." Example speaks louder than words, and your children are deeply affected by what they see in your life.

The devil wants to get mom to give up her teaching position at home and give all her time and energy to some other job that is less important and eternal. He offers her all kinds of pay and benefits and self-esteem. Once he gets you out of the picture, he's got lots of others lined up to do your job for you and teach your children what he wants them to be taught. Think of all the things they'll learn from television, rock music, cartoons, video games, public schools and humanism, perverts and queers, atheists and evolutionists... you get the picture.

SWITCHBOARD OPERATOR - COMMUNICATIONS EXPERT

I don't think I've heard anyone else mention this as an important aspect of a mother's ministry, but since I think it is, I'll be the first. One of the most important things I think I have to do in my family is to keep communication going between dad and kids, and sound an alert when I perceive a problem. I guess this stands out to me in my family especially since I am in a strategic position between a very masculine dad and very feminine teenage girls who could easily misunderstand or have a hard time finding common ground. On top of that, the dad in our family is sometimes long-distance for substantial periods of time, and even when we're all in the same location, we're often all busy and going in separate directions. I think my situation probably coincides with many moms whose husbands have a demanding work schedule, especially if their children also have plenty of outside activities.

Enter: Mom, the Switchboard Operator. She keeps everybody in the family in touch with everybody else. Since mom is already occupied with 'looking well to the ways of her household', it naturally follows that she's the one to keep dad informed, too. I am the one to dial the phone if I think the kids need to have a talk with dad, sometimes 'just because'. I need to let dad know about what's on their minds, things that are bothering them, attitudes that need to be addressed and corrected. I need to remind him about their holidays and special events, and let him know when they're in need of some extra attention. My most common statement in this regard is: "I think it's ___'s turn for a Daddy-date," because my husband enjoys spending that time with them, but doesn't always think of it because of all the other responsibilities on his mind. Mom's ministry will keep dad current and up-to-date on their activities and friendships and especially what I can see of their heart condition.

I also have a ministry in communication that goes in the other direction from Dad to kids. I am the self-appointed watchdog of family rules, especially about dress and music and boy-girl standards. I need to remind my kids about what pleases dad, what's unacceptable, and keep dad's influence present even when he's not.

It's also my job to build up dad to my kids, to talk about him in a positive light and remind my kids what he does for us and how much we have to be thankful for. If I have a gripe with him, my kids are not the people to confide in. The H oly Spirit's job is to promote and cultivate love, harmony, loyalty and unity, and that's my job, as well. I need to be using the fabric of every day family life to try to knit hearts together, and keep all relationships within our family close. It's also a matter of prayer to try to know when I'm needed to step in as mediator in the Father/child relationship, and when it's better to just step back and stay out of the way.

Mom, you're the switchboard operator in your family. Keep everybody in touch and informed and close in the family circle. Keep dad involved in your children's lives, and your children in contact with his influence.

COMFORTER - COUNSELOR

"But when the Comforter is come, whom I will send unto you from the Father, even the spirit of truth, which proceedeth from the Father, he shall testify of me." (John 15:26) "Nevertheless I tell you the truth; It is expedient for you that I go away: for if I go not away, the Comforter will not come unto you; but if I depart, I will send him unto you. And when he is come, he will reprove the world of sin, and of righteousness, and of judgment: .... Howbeit, when he, the Spirit of truth, is come, he will guide you into all truth: for he shall not speak of himself; but whatsoever he shall hear, that shall he speak, and he will shew you things to come. He shall glorify me: for he shall receive of mine, and shall shew it unto you." (John 16:7-8, 13-14)

60

A Closer Look at the Ministry of Mom

Only mom, who is there from beginning to end through all the ups and downs of life, can feel the hurts and provide comfort and encouragement to those closest to her heart like the Holy Spirit does. The Comforter is our *'paraclete'*, the one who comes alongside and bears us up. Mom is a comforter and sympathetic heart to all the growing pains her children face. She's the one who sees their life from the beginning, who sees all the growth and progress so far, who sees where they may have digressed a little bit and need to get back on track. Mom is the one with the sweetest dreams and highest hopes for their future happiness and usefulness inside the will of God, so she is immediately wary when she senses dangerous influences and temptations that they may not recognize. There's no one so unselfish and caring and concerned and sympathetic as a mom is. Abraham Lincoln's heartfelt statement agrees: "A mother's death is the first great heartache that her child will ever face without her."

INTERCESSOR

"Likewise, the Spirit also helpeth our infirmities: for we know not what we should pray for as we ought: but the Spirit itself maketh intercession for us with groanings which cannot be uttered. And he that searcheth the hearts knoweth what is the mind of the Spirit, because he maketh intercession for the saints according to the will of God." (*Romans 8:26-27*) The Holy Spirit is our prayer-partner who begs and pleads and intercedes at the throne of God for our every need. The Holy Spirit feels our burdens, hears our silent heart-cries, and experiences our pain. So much like the Holy Spirit, nobody can pray more fervently or lovingly for your child than mom.

Doesn't every child deserve to have someone to hold

61

him up before the throne of grace and beg for God's mercies and guidance in their behalf? If not you, then who? Who cares more than you do? Let's not get so busy with physical needs that we neglect the more important spiritual needs that our children have. No matter what else you do for your children, don't forget to pray.

Beyond that, so many things that we face in raising our children seem to find no other answer but to take it to the Lord. How comforting to know that, "When I've come to the end of myself -- my own strength, my own wisdom, my own patience -- I'm only at the beginning of God's." Lately as I've talked to friends and we've discussed our experiences in raising teenagers, I've found myself saying again and again, "They'll keep us praying, won't they?"

I know there are areas where I've fallen short in raising my children, and a few in particular where I'm aware of my absolute, utter, flat-on-my-face failure. Yet this is not one of those endeavors in which you can throw your hands in the air and say, "I give up!" You don't get to go back to the beginning and start over. This is my child's life, and I've got to do the best I can and pray for the Lord to do the best He can (which is much more than enough) from where we are right now. Thank the Lord that He's waiting to hear from us -- not just when we've succeeded and done our best. Even in the face of total failure, and maybe even some direct disobedience that has been detrimental to our children, the Lord waits to hear and answer our prayers with forgiveness, and power to change hearts and order circumstances and work miracles to bring our children back to Him and to His perfect will for their lives.

I'm convinced that a mother who spends plenty of time at the throne of grace, basking in the presence of the Lord, is the best mother any child could ever have. What kind of a mother would she be? God-fearing. Christ-honoring.

A Closer Look at the Ministry of Mom

Spirit-filled. Bible-centered. A good example. Loving. Kind. Unselfish. Patient. Joyful. Hard -working. Observant. Teaching. A good and loving wife.

No matter what books you read or what seminars you go to, they're going to tell you that these are the important qualities and characteristics that will make you a good mother. God says, "If you just pray daily and fervently, I want to use that time spent with Me to make you the best mother you can possibly be." I'm realizing more every day that no mother is really a good mother unless she is a praying mother.

How would godly, praying mothers affect the course of this nation? Napoleon Bonaparte said, "The future destiny of a child is the life's work of a mother. Let France have good mothers and she will have good sons." "When all is said, it is the mother, and the mother only, who is a better citizen than the soldier who fights for his country. The successful mother, the mother who does her part in rearing and training aright the boys and girls who are to be the men and women of the next generation, is of greater use to the community, and occupies, if she only would realize it, a more honorable as well as a more important position than any man it it. The mother is the one supreme asset of the national life. She is more important, by far, than the successful statesman, or businessman, or artist, or scientist." (Theodore Roosevelt) We've certainly lost that emphasis in America in this generation.

It would be easy to despair if I thought raising my kids for the Lord depended solely on me. I have to leave things in God's hands, realizing He knows I've tried to be a good mother even when I was failing. Since I'm God's Junior-Partner in this endeavor, I'm trusting Him to correct my boo-boos and help me go on from where I'm at now. I'm asking and trusting that my children will live their lives for

Him, and when they do, God will get all the glory, because I've already made more than enough mistakes to deserve any credit at all! I've proven I'm no expert so I don't expect to go down in history as the perfect mother.

Still I want my children to rest assured that they are in my prayers constantly. I wish I was faithful and fervent enough that the Lord just couldn't let one of them wander from Him. I'm not there yet, but that's what I want to strive for in my prayer-life as a mom.

In the past few years, I've taken it on myself to challenge ladies to see their lives and duties as a ministry of serving the Lord, and serving people for the Lord. I believe that with all of my heart. Mom, your ministry is just as important as the ministry of Dr. Roberson or Dr. Hyles or anyone else you'd like to name. I want to applaud you and encourage you for doing your best in serving God within your family, and I want to remind you too, if you're in need of a reminder.

While I was thinking these thoughts and getting ready to write this message, I heard a heart-wrenching story, and it all started with a pastor who lost his vision. He no longer had the same dream, the same dedication, the same enthusiasm, or the same realization of what God could and would do in response to his prayer and hard work. Once he lost his vision for his ministry, it wasn't long before he left his ministry altogether.

I asked myself the same questions I'm asking you. Have you lost your vision for your ministry? Ask God to renew your vision, your realization of it's importance, your love and commitment to your family and meeting their needs, your vision of what those children can become in the perfect will of God for their lives. When I asked that question, it became clear to me that I had lost my vision for this ministry in relation to raising a toddler. I had let some things slide and didn't apply or stretch myself because I was only looking at the temporary moment instead of the final goal. That's not how I once approached it. God convicted my heart, and I made a new commitment to do my best.

Where are you in this ministry? Are you in the hoping and planning stage, expecting a new baby or tearfully watching one asleep in the crib? Are you busy chasing preschoolers or answering a million why's that come with the primary years? Perhaps, like me, you're watching your junior or teenage children race headlong toward adulthood and praying all the while that they'll stay on track and become what God has planned for them. Even if all your children have grown and married and added grandchildren to your family picture, God has a loving ministry for you to perform in their lives.

By the way, I forgot to mention one very encouraging detail. Guaranteed success is available upon request! *"God is able to make all grace abound toward you, that you, having all sufficiency in all things, may abound unto every good work."* Proverbs 22:6 *"Train up a child in the way he should go, and when he is old he will not depart from it."* Philippians 4:13 *"I can do all things through Christ which strengtheneth me."*

I've probably found all of us somewhere in this scenario. Are you lost in the everyday details? Are you discouraged and despairing? Are you praying and trusting and laboring together with God in this important ministry? Let me challenge you again, as I've challenged myself, to give your all and do your utmost in this rewarding ministry of being a mother, the Holy Spirit of the home.

Manoah's Wife answered the Call to Motherhood with A Desire to Do God's Work in God's Way:

"Then Manoah intreated the LORD, and said, O my Lord, let the man of God which thou didst send come again unto us, and teach us what we shall do unto the child that shall be born...
And Manoah said, Now let thy words come to pass. How shall we order the child, and how shall we do unto him?"
Judges 13:8, 12

Chapter Six

Success In Motherhood!

This title is somewhat comical to me, because it makes me think of "Success In Crossword Puzzles", or "Success In Canning" or "Success In Real Estate." I mean, how does one of those categories compare with something as far-reaching and all-encompassing as the life's work of a wife and mother? Yet, I want to stick with that title and theme, because there's a definite idea that I'd like to convey.

'Success' is one of the favorite buzzwords of today's society. I don't think you could pick up any magazine or newspaper without finding at least one article promising the secrets to success in some area or endeavor. I know a great title for a book that would be sure to sell a billion copies. I'd call it "Successful Marriage, Successful Motherhood, Successful ME!" The only problem is, I have no idea what I would write inside the cover!

This 'success syndrome' is kind of like an invisible

burden that we all carry around with us, knowing that the world is watching us, and we're even keeping an eye on ourselves, expecting some elusive, indefinable results or accomplishments to materialize that will allow us to sigh in relief, knowing that we've attained success and not failure. I think it may be one of those rings the devil has designed, made it look virtuous, and then inserted one in the nose of every Christian so he can drag us around in the direction of his choice.

Yet the most important job and purpose for a lady is doing what God created her to do, being a wife and a mother. I truly want to be successful in that endeavor; I don't want to fail. But how in the world do you define success for a mom? What jobs or accomplishments appear on that checklist of responsibilities that promises if I can just scratch off each item as finished, then I'm a successful mom?

There must be some definite guidelines and instructions, or how would anyone ever determine success or failure, and how would they even know how to begin or which direction to go? We can never know if we're successful in God's eyes doing the job that God created us to do until we study and obey God's instructions concerning what a godly wife and mother is supposed to be and do.

Someone once said, "Failure is the best means by which a person can start over more intelligently." But in motherhood, you don't get to say, "Oops, that child was a total failure -- guess I'll start over." We have just one opportunity to raise each child that God entrusts to our care. We'd better find out what we're supposed to do and get God involved in it, too. It's the most important area in which to be successful, yet we're not sure how to measure success in this area.

Where is the measuring stick for success in

motherhood? Perhaps that's at least a fraction of the reason why so many moms have left their homes to pursue 'successful' careers -- at least they feel like they can fulfill the responsibilities and feel a sense of accomplishment rather than frustration, instead of devoting their entire lives to an area in which they never know if they're doing well or not. I mean, "If I'm going to fail in the area of home and family, at least let me succeed at something!" I really think that might be some of the underlying propaganda that the devil has used to take so many mothers out of their homes. Maybe a more accurate description would be to say that's the way the devil has managed to take home and family out of the hearts of so many mothers.

But success in any other vocation can never compensate for what a woman loses when she puts some other career first in her life, when home becomes just headquarters and hotel instead of the heart of the family. In the same measure that moms have left home for more 'successful' careers, the divorce rate, crime rate, juvenile delinquency rate, suicide rate, illegitimate birth rate, and drug and alcohol use by children and teenagers have risen astronomically. We need to find some answers before our families are included in those statistics.

How do you measure success? Image? Oh, brother, if anybody ever sees me balancing baby, laundry, telephone and computer before I've made it out of my bathrobe, I'm sure they won't tag me as a success! Paycheck? Well, if you're a stay-at-home mom, even if you're a part of a home-based business, there will be days when it feels like the financial crunch is squeezing the breath right out of you. Feeling or looking successful?   Is that before or after your two year old has an accident in your lap, and in the unexpected rush you don't quite have time to yank the rollers out of your hair and brush it, too? I AM trying to be funny, but I think you know that if you're depending on any or all of those gauges to measure your success as a mom, you're in for a disappointment.

The devil has stolen away our pleasure and pride in the glorious vocation to which we've been called as wives and mothers. I received this little piece in my e-mail that describes one woman's frustration with society's view of her role as a mom.

I'm Just a Mother?

A few months ago, when I was picking up the children at school, another mother that I knew well, rushed up to me. Emily was fuming with indignation. "Do you know what you and I are?" she demanded.

Before I could answer, and I didn't really have one handy, she blurted out the reason for her question. It seemed she had just returned from renewing her driver's license at the County Clerk's office. Asked by the woman recorder to state her "occupation," Emily had hesitated, uncertain how to classify herself. "What I mean is," explained the recorder, "Do you have a job, or are you just a ......?"

"Of course I have a job," snapped Emily. "I'm a mother."

"We don't list 'mother' as an occupation, 'housewife' covers it," said the recorder emphatically.

I forgot all about her story until one day I found myself in the same situation, this time at our own Town Hall. The Clerk was obviously a career woman, poised, efficient, and possessed of a high-sounding title, like "Official Interrogator" or "Town Registrar."

"And what is your occupation?" she probed.

What made me say it, I do not know. The words simply popped out. "I'm a Research Associate in the field of Child

Development and Human Relations."

The clerk paused, ball-point pen frozen in mid-air, and looked up as though she had not heard right. I repeated the title slowly, emphasizing the most significant words.

Then I stared with wonder as my pompous pronouncement was written in bold, black ink on the official questionnaire.

"Might I ask," said the clerk with new interest, "just what you do in your field?"

Coolly, without any trace of fluster in my voice, I heard myself reply, "I have a continuing program of research (what mother doesn't) in the laboratory and in the field (normally I would have said indoors and out).

I'm working for my Masters (the whole family) and already have four credits (all daughters). Of course, the job is one of the most demanding in the humanities (any mother care to disagree?) and I often work 14 hours a day (24 is more like it). But the job is more challenging than most run-of-the-mill careers and the rewards are in satisfaction rather than just money."

There was an increasing note of respect in the clerk's voice as she completed the form, stood up, and personally ushered me to the door.

As I drove into our driveway buoyed up by my glamorous new career, I was greeted by my lab assistants-- ages 13, 7, and 3. And upstairs, I could hear our new experimental model (six months) in the child-development program, testing out a new vocal pattern.

I felt triumphant. I had scored one on the bureaucracy. And I had gone down on the official records as someone more distinguished and indispensable to mankind than "just another......"

Home...what a glorious career.

Mission: Motherhood

The world measures success by how big the paycheck, how fine the house, how new the car, how stylish the clothing, and how impressive the job title. We know that's not God's way, but HOW <u>DO</u> YOU MEASURE SUCCESS? (Can you hear my frantic tone yet?) America's moms have fallen victim to the empty promises of success that the devil whispers in our ears, and we're paying a high price in heartbreak, wrecked lives, shattered dreams, and broken families that is due, at least in part, to mothers leaving the vocation of motherhood to pursue other less important careers.

Now let me say, I know that not every family's situation is the same, and I'm not judgmental or critical about all women who hold any type of job, because I know that the world has reconstructed our economy to the point where many women don't have a choice. Whether or not you can or should have a job outside your home is something that can only be decided by the Lord and your husband and yourself. But I am saying that if you go to a job outside your home, it needs to be your sideline pursuit; that home and family needs to stay in first place in your heart, your goals, your effort and your time.

There is no other job that is as eternal or as rewarding as investing your life in the children that God has entrusted to you. That paycheck may last a week, and if you put it in the bank and don't cash in on its benefits, you might even hang on to it a few years. But there is no monetary replacement equal to the value of a loving, godly family with dad as the head and mom as the heart. No paycheck can equal the blessings that God intended for a truly successful mother.

By the way, how can you put a price tag on things like: a slobbery kiss? the fragrance of a just-bathed baby? your toddler's first "I wuv oo" and "Mommy's pwetty"? your first Crayola designer greeting card? your daughter's first lopsided cake? your son's first big catch? your first bouquet of dandelions? your first breakfast in bed consisting of soggy cereal, burned toast and coffee complete with the grounds?

I've often thought tearfully of the young mothers who come home from work to hear the baby-sitter say, "The baby took his first steps today," or "The baby said her first words today." Thank the Lord, though I've always been busy during my years of motherhood and juggled several responsibilities, at least I've been able to keep my children with me, and not miss all those momentous occasions. It's very true that there are some things that money can't buy.

"Who can find a virtuous woman? for her price is far above rubies." (Proverbs 31:10) Proverbs 31 is the chapter that outlines the accomplishments of God's ideal woman, and all of her life centers around her home and family. The text in Titus chapter two gives us a brief but powerful outline of what God expects from a wife and mother. *"That they may teach the young women to be sober, to love their husbands, to love their children, To be discreet, chaste, keepers at home, good, obedient to their own husbands, that the word of God be not blasphemed." (Titus 2:4-5)* There is a lot that can be said about those few instructions, and I have talked about them in a little more detail in some other issues.

But let me at least point out that the first and foremost responsibility of a mother is love -- to love our husbands and love our children. Sounds easy, doesn't it? I mean, we're supposedly the mushy, gushy gender who can think about nothing else but love and romance, right?

Yes, but what about when our loved ones aren't so lovable? Our responsibility to love those in our family does not decrease even a fraction of a percent, no matter what kind of treatment we may get in return. Now we're getting down to the hard part. Love comes first, before interior decorating and winning the Yard of the Month or Betty Crocker cooking award. No matter how many responsibilities you may have received along with motherhood, the very first and most important one is to love your family.

Paul said, *"Though I speak with the tongues of men and of angels, and have not charity, I am become as sounding brass, or a tinkling cymbal. And though I have the gift of prophecy, and understand all mysteries, and all knowledge; and though I have all faith, so that I could remove mountains, and have not charity, I am nothing. And though I bestow all my goods to feed the poor, and though I give my body to be burned, and have not charity, it profiteth me nothing."* (I Corinthians 13) No matter how high my attainments may soar, even in spiritual matters such as teaching, Bible knowledge, faith, generosity, or self-denial, without love, it means nothing at all. Love is the first requirement to be a successful mom.

I'm going to meddle a little deeper here, the love that's required of us is not just emotional attachment or fulfillment. Real love is an action, not an emotion. Scripturally, love is doing what is best for the object of my love, regardless of personal expense. *"For God so loved the world that he gave his only begotten Son..."*

God's love prompted Him to give without limits, and to meet the great need of those of us whom He loves, no matter what it took. Love is not doing only what gives me or my family a warm emotion. It's not just doing what my loved one thinks is best for them, because sometimes what is really best is in total opposition to their plans and desires. It's not just doing what is best for my husband and children until it becomes too costly or too demanding or too painful. It is doing what God says is best for my family, at all costs, at all times.

What is the limit on love? *"For God so loved the world that he gave his only begotten Son..."* That's where we learn the definition of love, and it's also where we find the demands. Love demands our all. Love goes as far as necessary, pays as much as it may cost, suffers to the end, waits long enough, however long that may be. Whatever action love requires, there is no limit to how far, how long, how much, or how deep. Real love will pay as much as it costs, no matter how far that may take me.

Real love is a self-giving love. Paul was speaking to his converts, his children in the Lord, about the fact that he loved them not for what he could get from them, but for themselves. *"And I will very gladly spend and be spent for you; though the more abundantly I love you, the less I be loved."* (II Corinthians 12:15) Real love is giving without limitations and going the extra mile with no strings attached, loving our family regardless of whether or not we are receiving their love in return.

Sound impossible? Well, it might be, except that God is the Author and Fountainhead of love, as well as life, and He makes it possible for us to tap into His resources and love with the love of God. Again, "God's commands are His enablings." Because God commands love, He also supplies us with all that is necessary to obey His command.

God gave us several other areas to work on in Titus 2:4-5. He said that we are to love our husbands and children. We've been commanded to be discreet and chaste. In a nutshell, He's commanding us to be morally clean, pure, faithful and above reproach in our lives, our testimonies, and our relationships with all others.

The next item is to be 'keepers at home.' That means that home is my life's work, and my life and my work are centered around my home. Just as the final responsibility for providing for the family rests with the man, husbands are more than welcome to help out with home responsibilities, and there are many times and situations when they should. But when it comes to being a keeper at home, ladies, the buck stops here. The final responsibility for that job Scripturally belongs to the wife and mother in the home.

May I add that being a home-keeper is more than just being a housekeeper? My home consists more importantly of the people who live in my home than in the building that houses us. Meeting needs -- spiritual and emotional needs as well as the physical ones -- is even more important than keeping up with the cleaning and maintenance of the house we live in.

The next requirement is a good one. That's it; be good! I learned by looking a little deeper that it means being good in what I am as well as in what I do. God is good; He is incapable of being anything but good, beneficial, loving, and caring. In growing to be more godly or God-like, I am allowing the Lord to duplicate these qualities in me so that my life affects all those around me with the same beneficial goodness.

'Obedient to their own husbands' is the next item on the list, and no, we can't just skip it! I think it would be correct to say that a wife's obedience and submission are two sides to the same coin. While obedience is doing the will of another, submission is placing your own will under the will of another. Sin has made this a tough pill for us to swallow, and our own pride and self-will wants to assert itself and say, "Nothing doing!" But if we could get back to the life God had planned for us before sin came on the scene, it would be a piece of cake instead!

You see, if I was surrendered to doing the will of God and my husband was surrendered to doing the will of God, then when God commanded me to submit, obey and follow the leadership of my husband, I would simply be following my husband in the same direction that I already planned to go! But I can't wait until my husband tells me to do what I want to do before I start obeying this command from God. I am either trying my best to submit to my husband, or I am disobedient to God -- I'll have to choose between the two.

That final phrase in verse five is the one that first riveted my attention to this passage and took my breath away. ***"That the word of God be not blasphemed."*** We're not talking about the words that I say here. We're talking specifically about how I live my life as a wife and a mother. The very idea that I could be guilty of blasphemy against God's Word just by my actions and lifestyle was a very sobering thought that made me stop and ponder for quite a while. How vital is it that I obey the Lord in these few areas we've just mentioned from Titus chapter two? It must be pretty important if failure to do so is equal to blasphemy.

It sounds to me like God deems the job of a wife and mother as a pretty important one. Success or failure in my job as a wife and mother is going to have a greater impact on the rest of my life than what the world calls success in any other area.

Mission: Motherhood

Success In Motherhood!
Part Two

When I was first preparing for this message, I came across this in my e-mail, and I couldn't help laughing hysterically while having sympathy pains for the poor mother! I'm certain that, just like me, she's had plenty of days when she didn't feel very successful!

THINGS I'VE LEARNED FROM MY CHILDREN
(HONEST AND NO KIDDING):
1. A king size waterbed holds enough water to fill a 2000 sq. foot house 4 inches deep.
2. If you spray hair spray on dust bunnies and run over them with roller blades, they can ignite.
3. A 3-year-old's voice is louder than 200 adults in a crowded restaurant.
4. If you hook a dog leash over a ceiling fan, the motor is not strong enough to rotate a 42 pound boy wearing Batman underwear and a superman-cape. It is strong enough, however, to spread paint on all four walls of a 20 by 20 foot room.
5. You should not throw baseballs up when the ceiling fan is on. When using the ceiling fan as a bat, you have to throw the ball up a few times before you get a hit. A ceiling fan can

hit a baseball a long way.

6. The glass in windows (even double pane) doesn't stop a baseball hit by a ceiling fan.

7. When you hear the toilet flush and the words "Uh-oh", it's already too late.

8. Brake fluid mixed with Clorox makes smoke, and lots of it.

9. A six year old can start a fire with a flint rock even though a 36-year-old man says they can only do it in the movies. A magnifying glass can start a fire even on an overcast day.

10. Certain Lego's will pass through the digestive tract of a four year old.

11. Play Dough and Microwave should never be used in the same sentence.

12. Super glue is forever.

13. No matter how much Jell-O you put in a swimming pool, you still can't walk on water.

14. Pool filters do not like Jell-O.

15. VCR's do not eject Peanut Butter & Jelly sandwiches even though TV commercials show they do.

16. Garbage bags do not make good parachutes.

17. Marbles in gas tanks make lots of noise when driving.

18. You probably do not want to know what that odor is.

19. Always look in the oven before you turn it on. Plastic toys do not like ovens.

20. The fire department in Austin, Texas has a 5 minute response time.

21. The spin cycle on the washing machine does not make earth worms dizzy. It will however make cats dizzy.

22. Basketballs and soccer balls will not get clean in the washer and will not get dry in the dryer...they only make noise.

23. Cats can throw up twice their body weight when dizzy.

24. Eggs will not incubate in the microwave.

25. Milk shakes just cannot be made in the clothes dryer, even on 'air only!

Throughout most of your years of raising children, it's usually difficult, if not impossible, to 'feel successful'. You know, to feel like you're accomplishing something, you're headed somewhere, and you're making some definite, measurable progress. Maybe one of the reasons is because a day's work is never finished when the day is finished! Motherhood is not set up with a schedule of awards, you know, the kind where you complete this workbook and receive this certificate. It's more like the efforts of a mountain-climber. You're not going to hear much about how well you're doing until you've reached the end of the climb, so I guess we'd better start looking for some other sources of encouragement and motivation!

When I first began to file through my brain looking for ideas and principles about success on the homefront, these were the first two words I came up with -- OBEDIENCE AND ENJOYMENT. At first they seemed totally unrelated, but the longer I mulled over my thoughts and ideas, they seemed to belong together. By the time I had finished my musing session, I came to the conclusion that putting these two ideas together was not my original idea at all, because thousands of years ago the Lord linked these two principles in the Scriptures and called it "Godliness With Contentment." Each of these items, obedience and enjoyment, is priceless and powerful. But together they unite to generate a power 10 times greater than either of them produce alone, valued 10 times as high as the worth of each one singly.

Obedience is step one to success. In fact, obedience is probably 99 steps out of 100. It's not feeling successful, looking successful, or acting successful. It's just doing what God said to do. I heard someone say many years ago that, "Success is finding the will of God and doing it for a lifetime." I believe that to be true. That simplifies our dilemma a great deal, wouldn't you agree? The way to measure success in any area, especially marriage and motherhood, is just to find out what God said to do, and then do it faithfully for a lifetime to the best of my ability. If you're obedient, you're a success!

My husband often preaches this principle as it relates to soulwinning. Success is not measured in results but in obedience, not in how many souls you win, but how faithfully you go and present the Gospel. So does that mean that you are a successful soulwinner without results? No, it just means you are a success BEFORE the results. Because we're following God's program and claiming God's promises, the results are guaranteed. Faithfulness is the secret ingredient. However, alot of people concede defeat and quit before they ever see the fruit. That's really the only way that you can fail in the will of God.

This truth applies to us as mothers also. God has given us a program to follow in the Bible, and most of the ladies reading this are genuinely trying. Since the devil can't prevent us from succeeding if we're faithful and obedient, then he works to undermine our faithfulness and obedience, and to discourage us into quitting before the job is finished and we see the results.

The whole Bible abounds with principles and commands concerning childtraining, and the book of Proverbs in particular gives some pretty specific instruction. We are given God's promise, as well. *"Train up a child in the way he should go: and when he is old, he will not depart from it." (Proverbs 22:6)* We can trust and obey and cling to God's promise, knowing that success in motherhood doesn't depend on my expertise in motherhood, but just obeying God's commands and trusting

Him to keep His promise.

I sat in a Sunday School class years ago and heard the teacher say, "I know the Bible says if you train your children right, then when they grow up, they won't depart from it. But I just don't believe that's so, because my children all went astray from what I taught them." I promise, if I had worn false teeth, they would have been laying broken on the floor! I couldn't believe she was saying that because her children disappointed her, then the Bible wasn't true. I vowed to the Lord that day that if my children disappoint me someday, I will shoulder the blame, and I'll never discredit the Bible or the Lord based on my successes or failures as a mother.

Now I must confide in you that many years have passed, and there have been moments when I thought God might be planning to make me prove my point, and I was definitely failing as a mother. But I still accept by faith that God cannot fail, so any failure with my children must be on my part and not on His part.

Success IS obedience. Noah was used to preach to the whole world at a pivotal point in history, yet we know of only eight converts he had to show for a whole lifetime -- his own family. Some people wouldn't call him successful, but God said that Noah found grace in the eyes of the Lord. Noah succeeded because he obeyed.

Mary volunteered her life to God's service and laid down all of her own dreams and plans for the plan of God. When the angel announced that she had been chosen to be the mother of the Promised Saviour, she said, *"Behold the handmaid of the Lord; be it unto me according to thy word."* You would think that such an important woman in history would be surrounded with the mysterious aura of successful image, but I don't think that was the case. I believe that, instead, she was misunderstood and maligned by the people around her throughout most of her life. How could people continue to doubt the identity of Jesus Christ as the Messiah unless they believed or at least suspected her to be less than respectable? For 33 long years after she volunteered for this service to God that reached to all times and places, she didn't get to see the truth of what she knew in her heart -- I guess you might say she was walking by faith and not by sight! I believe that the resurrection of Christ might have been the first public affirmation she ever had of who she was and what God had called her to do.

Hannah was seen by the world around her as poor, pitied, and picked on -- the barren 'other wife.' In that culture, motherhood was a woman's primary source of identity, and to be childless was a social heartache as well as a personal one. So consumed was she with her yearning to have a child, that she was willing to give up her heart's desire when she finally received it, and sent young Samuel to serve God at the Temple. But God in His goodness gave her five more children to love. I think you could find many examples in the Bible of people who may not have looked very successful by the world's standard, yet in God's book they are a success. Eternity will know their names, though society may not.

I heard someone say recently that any person's life could produce an outstanding or terrible SNAPSHOT, depending on which moment it happened to be taken. As a matter of fact, you might be more likely to see the impressive snapshot of someone who's 'posing,' or living for the perception of others to be seen of men, while the person who's just quietly doing their job might not look quite as impressive at any single moment. But you're talking about an entirely different ballgame when you look at a VIDEO, and watch it from beginning to end.

It's not over until it's over! The video is not complete,

friend, until the Judgment Seat of Christ, so don't decide that you've lost the ball game in the first quarter! This snapshot/video idea inspired me to get my eyes off of the discouraging snapshots, of myself as well as others, and take into consideration that there is a whole video to be viewed before any opinion is formed about whether my life or someone else's is to be pronounced as a success or a failure. Only God is truly qualified to judge success or lack of it.

It doesn't really matter how it looks to anybody right now. Depend on God to keep his promise, and trust Him for the end result. We need to get our heads out of this world's 'rat-race mentality' and adopt God's measuring stick as our own. Obedience equals success.

Success In Motherhood!

Part Three

I made the statement earlier that, in motherhood, obedience is 99% of success, and I still think that's true when I'm thinking about the subject of obedience. But when I look at this other item, I'm struck by it's weighty importance, as well. So if I'm anywhere near correct in saying that it's only one percent of the whole, let me stress that it is a mighty important one percent!

That final penny that makes up the whole dollar of success in motherhood is to add contentment to your complete and faithful obedience. I'm convinced that much of the heartache and tragedy we're seeing on the homefront today stems from the discontentment and dissatisfaction of American wives and mothers, and more specifically, Christian wives and mothers. We've allowed the devil to dangle his pretty package before our noses wrapped in all the world's shiny glitz and glitter, and we've believed him about the contents that await us inside.

But just like Eve found out, you can't believe the father of lies -- he'll lie to you every time. The devil will promise you anything that appeals to you, but he never even intends to keep any of the promises that he makes. Why do we keep listening to him?

85

Mission: Motherhood

I'm as sure as I am that my name is Cathy Corle that the devil has carefully orchestrated his plan to project this image of 'the successful woman' unceasingly before our eyes, and to constantly tempt and suggest and plant thoughts in our minds to make us think that elusive phantom is exactly what we want to become. Maybe it's alot like the role-playing games that kids get so addicted to; we want to assume this image and identity and live this 'charmed existence' (so the devil would like us to think) of success, prosperity, glamour, freedom, fulfillment, and enjoyment.

My husband just led a lady to the Lord on a plane, and was sharing with me all her heartache. She's in a high-paid executive position and has been for many years. She has everything that money can buy. While she's been making money and climbing the corporate ladder for the last 20 years, her family has spent much of the time without a wife and mother in the home.

Since her husband was much better acquainted with the secretary of his small business who he had spent so much time with while he became more and more a stranger to his own wife, he decided he'd be happier married to the woman he actually lives with the most. The oldest children have already wrecked their lives in the world and gone their own way.

There is one boy still in high school, and constantly bombarded with the rock music, drugs, sex, and gang influence around him every day. She confided in my husband after she got saved that she thought she ought to sell her picture-perfect California home, take a year's sabbatical from work, and spend this last year with her youngest son before he graduates. The world would laud this woman as a shining example of success and wealth for females everywhere to follow, but I don't think she would

86

give you the same advice.

The devil will feed you a constant stream of, "You would be happy if..." Let me remind you again that you will only be happy if you unplug your receiving unit to all the lies of the world, the flesh and the devil and decide once and for all that there is absolutely no chance of happiness in following the plan and program they have designed for your life. You will only be happy if you find and follow whole-heartedly the plan that God has for your life.

Blessed, or happy, or approved of God, is the man or woman who shuns the advice of the ungodly, but his or her delight is in the law of the Lord, and in His law do they meditate and obey day and night. That word 'blessed' in Psalm one means both 'happy' and 'approved of God'. My husband's sermon well illustrates that only what God approves can make a person happy. So not just success, but also happiness, contentment, and fulfillment are wrapped up in finding the will of God and doing it for a lifetime.

It's been said that, "Contentment is the art of enjoying what you have." But for most of the world, it's a lost art. Most people with a family to treasure don't see the true value of what they have until they've already lost it. Contentment is not found in having everything you want. Contentment equals wanting everything that you have.

We tend to think of contentment only in financial terms, but since the most important things in life can't be bought with money, we need to widen our scope and look at the value of what we have that doesn't translate into dollar signs. At Mother's Day I reminded ladies, "If you have a mother, you are blessed. If you are a mother, you are very blessed. If you have a mother and are a mother, you are doubly blessed. But if you have the legacy of loving family in your past, a godly marriage and family in your present and the continuing anticipation of close family ties with loving parents, loving husband, and precious children sent from God, their future spouses and children, then you are an immeasurably rich woman.

Contentment is an important ingredient in success at home. Contentment with our role, with our duties, with our schedule, with our homes and belongings and with our finances. Contentment is actually submission -- saying, "This is what my Heavenly Father chose for me, and I have chosen to be happy with it." We need to get content with the will of God for us as wives and mothers. We've been given the command, *"Let your conversation be without covetousness; and be content with such things as ye have: for he hath said, I will never leave thee, nor forsake thee."* *(Hebrews 13:5)* When we have the Lord, we have everything.

It's been said that the best thing you can give to your children is to be madly in love with their daddy, and building your marriage is the foundation for raising your children. Probably the area where Satan works hardest to stir up discontentment is in our marriages. "But I didn't expect marriage to be like this. I got married expecting love and romance and emotional support and closeness, but look what I got instead!"

Like Eve in the Garden, we're in danger, because we're constantly focusing on the one thing that we don't have, while ignoring all the wonderful things that we do have. Eve had forgotten about all the countless lovely trees and delicious fruits that were available to her because she allowed her attention to focus on the one that God had labeled 'off-limits.' How many women have wrecked their marriages and children in the same way? I wonder if there's a calculator that could count that high?

If you're having trouble remembering how much you have to be thankful for and content with, then I challenge you to remember that there are lots of women who would be more than happy to have a husband just like yours. Some ladies watch from afar to see a husband that is faithful, that works hard, pays the bills, shoulders the responsibility for the family, that is a good, faithful, honest man of integrity and says, "Wish I had one of those." If you look at your marriage through the eyes of someone else, you might see that you have a great deal for which to be thankful. It's imperative to realize that the devil is the one working so hard to keep your eyes off of what you do have and focused on what you don't have in order to keep you discontented.

Obedience plus enjoyment, which God has labeled "Godliness With Contentment," is the formula for success in motherhood as well as any other area of life. I've spent all my time stressing the importance of doing our job as mothers and being happy in it, instead of really getting into the job description, or God's commands to wives and mothers. But we've gone over that part often in the past, and most of us already have a pretty good idea of what we're supposed to be doing. I thought we need to concentrate on WHY we should be doing it for a change.

But before we're done, I do want to inject this thought about a mother's job. Let's use the same 'take-off runway' as our 'landing strip.' Success is finding the will of God and doing it for a lifetime, and that's just as true for my children as it is for me. Since I firmly believe that God has a purpose for each child, a specific plan for their lives and futures, then my purpose as a mom is to help them find and fulfill that purpose. Throughout their growing up years I can change hats and be coach, cheerleader, guide, medic, counselor and helper in their success so that they can find the will of God for their lives and get started on doing the will of God faithfully for the rest of their lives.

That's why all the things that we already know are

important have such importance in childtraining. Character building, Bible reading, prayer, faithful church attendance, honesty and integrity, obedience. Those are all elements of their success. I can contribute to that success through encouragement, prayer, believing in them, providing godly advice and leadership, and by being an example of obedience to God.

"This book of the law shall not depart out of thy mouth; but thou shalt meditate therein day and night, that thou mayest observe to do according to all that is written therein: for then thou shalt make thy way prosperous, and then thou shalt have good success. Have not I commanded thee? Be strong and of a good courage; be not afraid, neither be thou dismayed: for the Lord thy God is with thee whithersoever thou goest." (Joshua 1:8-9) I couldn't very well attempt to give my thoughts on 'Success in Motherhood' without pointing you to the only promise in the Bible that contains the word 'success.'

Success is inseparably linked to my relationship to the Word of God. We need to get in the Bible, get our children in the Bible, and get the Bible into them. And since 'the Lord thy God is with thee whithersoever thou goest,' then I need to remember that the presence and power of God is available and accessible in my quest for success in this most important endeavor of raising a family.

I told a friend of mine, Loretta Walker, that I spent much of my early years in the ministry as a preacher's wife and young mother frustrated about 'success.' I was on the road, living in an RV, going to church services every evening, schooling my children during the day, and busy, busy, busy. I'd see all these articles and hear all these messages about promised success, and it seemed like such an unattainable prize, always in sight and just beyond my reach. I said, "I stayed so upset with myself that I couldn't concentrate on success when all my time and effort was spent on SURVIVAL, until one day I came to the glorious conclusion that survival IS success. If I survive, then I've succeeded!" The day I realized that was a great day for me!

A successful mom is a needmeeter, so she's flexible, adjusting to needs of her family that are present right now. That will change with toddlers, fifth-graders, sophomores and college age kids. It's not hitting the ball out of the batting machine at practice, but playing the one that gets pitched to you in the real game that counts! More specifically, it's not making cookies and changing diapers on a doll in home-ec class, but dealing with a real one that cries and spits up and keeps you awake at night. This is the real thing, and it doesn't always line up with the organized schedule that you planned or the list of do's and don'ts that you copied down in someone's class.

Though we're given the same basic guidelines and commands, every mom's job is as unique and individual as her husband and children, and their ministry or circumstances. We do ourselves a favor when we learn to expect the unexpected and do the best we can at present with what and who we have to deal with right now. "What does the Lord want me to do right now in this situation, and which one of these needs is the first priority?" It's a constantly changing, adjusting, evaluating process, but hey, that's why management is such a high-paying career!

By the way, success has its rewards. Motherhood is the highest paying career in the world, but it doesn't compute in dollars and cents. *"Her children rise up and call her blessed."* God has designed every realm of life so that, when you give your best, you'll receive God's best. What could be a more appropriate reward for a dedicated mother than deep and abiding love from those you love the most. Honor and a special place in the hearts of the most important people in the world to you. Blessings innumerable that multiply day by day. Children whose lives you are proud of and who will continue to be the nearest and dearest friends of our lives. That sounds like a paycheck worth pursuing!

I said at the beginning that we don't have the luxury of failure and starting over in motherhood. That seems to leave me in a frightening position, but I have some good news. *"For we are labourers together with God..."* in our life's work as a mother, just as in soulwinning or any other important endeavor that God commands and calls us to fulfill. I find some relief in being the 'Junior Partner,' and knowing that God is really the One in charge here, since He has all the wisdom I lack, and He has the power and ability and opportunity to correct some of my mistakes, as well.

In doing the work God calls you to, it's important to do it in His power, in cooperation with His Holy Spirit, following His guidance, working in His strength. I'm not supposed to do God's will by following my own plan and doing things my own way. Paul commented on his service to God by saying, *"Whereunto I also labour, striving according to his working, which worketh in me mightily."* *(Colossians 1:29)* I need to get in cooperation with the Lord since it's His work and His will that I'm trying to accomplish anyway!

I already know I can't do it on my own. I've proven my own ability for failure over and over again. Even in the area of motherhood, I've found myself on my face before God many times crying out for His intervention to compensate for my inability and stupidity. My safety net for success has become the marriage of John 15:5 and Philippians 4:13! *"...Without me ye can do nothing"* but *"I can do all things through Christ which strengtheneth me."*

If we'll obey, and be content, and work together in

cooperation with the Lord, and try to the best of our ability to raise our children GOD's way, being the kind of Christian mother God wants them to have **WE CANNOT FAIL**. As is true in any endeavor, I must work like everything depends on me, and pray like everything depends on God.

I've had many experiences of fear and trepidation over whether or not I'll be a success in motherhood, but I've decided to wait until the judgment seat of Christ instead of putting a label on myself today! My children are not yet grown, and have not yet made all of their life's decisions. When you've invested as much of your life in them as you must in order to be a mother, then that's a scary thing, knowing that they can use their free will to go the wrong way and break your heart.

But I'm excited about the promises of God that we've looked at, and I'm more encouraged than ever before (only because the Lord promised and can't fail) that success in motherhood is attainable, even for me! Though you might not have realized it, I've just been 'encouraging myself in the Lord,' and letting you come along for the ride! I hope that something I've said in this long conversation I've been having with myself will be just the thing to encourage your heart today, as well.

Though it's a far cry from the world's image of success, all of God's promises of triumph and victory are available and powerful for us today, even those of us who are named 'Mom.' By following His instructions, praying for His guidance, acting in His power, and loving our families with His limitless 'agape' love, we can and WILL attain that goal of Success In Motherhood.

Hannah answered the Call to Motherhood by Giving Her Child's Life to the Lord:

"And she vowed a vow, and said, O LORD of hosts, if thou wilt indeed look on the affliction of thine handmaid, and ... wilt give unto thine handmaid a man child, then I will give him unto the LORD all the days of his life... And when she had weaned him, she took him up with her... and brought him unto the house of the LORD in Shiloh: and the child was young...

For this child I prayed; and the LORD hath given me my petition which I asked of him:"

1 Samuel 1:11, 24, 27

IF YOU WERE TO DIE TODAY, ARE YOU 100% SURE THAT YOU WOULD GO TO HEAVEN?

If you could know that, you would want to, wouldn't you?
Please take a few moments and let me share with you how the Bible says that you can know...

"Wherefore, as by one man sin entered into the world, and death by sin: and so death passed upon all men, for that all have sinned:" (Romans 5:12) The one thing that stands between us and going to Heaven when we die is our sin -- and God said that ALL have sinned. He didn't leave anyone out.

If I'm going to be honest with myself, I must admit that I am included. I am a sinner first of all because I inherited a sinful nature from Adam that has been passed down to me. I am a sinner also because I have disobeyed the clear

95

commands of God. Just as it only takes one instance of stealing to make me a thief, it takes only one sin to make me a sinner. There are no 'good sinners' or 'bad sinners' in the eyes of God -- we all stand guilty before Him, and unworthy of Heaven.

The Bible says that there is a penalty for sin -- DEATH. *"...and so death passed upon all men, for that all have sinned." (Romans 5:12) "For the wages of sin is death..." (Romans 6:23)* You cannot pay for sin by going to church or being baptized or doing good deeds or keeping commandments. The only payment that will clear your account is death. This is not just a physical death. The Bible is clear that after the body dies, there is a second death or a spiritual death.

"But the fearful, and unbelieving, and the abominable, and murderers, and whoremongers, and sorcerers, and idolaters, and all liars, shall have their part in the lake which burneth with fire and brimstone which is the second death." (Revelation 21:8) The Bible is clear that if we must pay the price for our sin, we must suffer a second death forever in the lake of fire called Hell. No other payment that we can make would pay the price, because the wages of sin is death.

God loves us so much that He did not want us to go to Hell, even though we deserve to do so. Yet He would not be just and righteous if He allowed us to go to Heaven with our sin, just as a judge would be unjust to let a murderer go free just because it was someone he knew and loved. Sin must be paid for. There is only one way for our sin to be paid for without you and I spending all eternity in the torment of Hell: to let Someone else pay the price for us.

"For God so loved the world, that he gave his only begotten Son, that whosoever believeth in him should not perish, but have everlasting life." (John 3:16) God

Plan of Salvation

allowed His Son, Jesus Christ, to suffer and die in our place to pay the price of death that we owe. We do not need to do anything to earn it, we must simply receive the salvation that Jesus paid for with His blood. *"But as many as received him, to them gave he power to become the sons of God, even to them that believe on his name:"* *(John 1:12)* If we will receive Jesus and His death on the cross as payment for our sins, He has promised to receive us into His family as a child of God.

"Behold, I stand at the door, and knock: if any man hear my voice, and open the door, I will come in to him..." *(Revelation 3:20)* Receiving Christ is as simple as opening the door and inviting someone in. Christ stands ready to come into your heart, forgive your sins, and make you a child of God. But He will only come by invitation. Won't you bow your head right now, wherever you are, and invite the Lord Jesus Christ to come in?

Lord Jesus,
I know that I am a sinner, and that
I deserve to go to Hell. Please
forgive me and come into my heart
right now. I'm trusting You to make
me a child of God, to take me to
Heaven when I die, and to help me
live the rest of my life for You.
Thank You for saving me.
In Jesus' name, Amen

Mission: Motherhood

If you sincerely prayed that prayer and asked the Lord to save you, He said, *"...I will come in."* That's not a maybe. He promised that He would. If you died right now with Christ in your heart, where would you go? To Heaven! If you had died before you asked Christ into your heart, where would you have gone? The difference between Heaven and Hell is the Lord Jesus Christ living within, Who died to pay the price of our sin.

Now that Christ lives in your heart, He has promised that He will never leave. *"...for he hath said, I will never leave thee, nor forsake thee."* No matter when you die, Christ will still be in your heart as He promised, so Heaven is as sure as if you were already there.

God does expect us to obey Him after we become His children, and the very first command that He gives is found in Acts 2:38. *"...Repent, and be baptized every one of you..."* Repentance takes place within, when I turn away from sin and self and turn to Christ as my Saviour. Baptism is the outward sign of what has happened in my heart -- a picture of the death, burial and resurrection of Jesus. Immediately after we get saved, God expects us to be baptized and show the world that we belong to Him.

If you have received Christ into your heart as a result of reading this book, please write and let us know. We'd like to send you a free copy of GROWING UP IN GOD'S FAMILY and LIVING UP TO YOUR NAME.

• • • • • • • •

Dr. Dennis Corle, Evangelist
Revival Fires!
P. O. Box 245
Claysburg, PA 16625
814-239-2813

98